At Issue

| Designer Babies

Other Books in the At Issue Series:

At Issue

Designer Babies

Clay Farris Naff

GREENHAVEN PRESS
A part of Gale, Cengage Learning

Detroit • New York • San Francisco • New Haven, Conn • Waterville, Maine • London

GALE
CENGAGE Learning

Elizabeth Des Chenes, *Director, Publishing Solutions*

© 2013 Greenhaven Press, a part of Gale, Cengage Learning

Gale and Greenhaven Press are registered trademarks used herein under license.

For more information, contact:
Greenhaven Press
27500 Drake Rd.
Farmington Hills, MI 48331-3535
Or you can visit our Internet site at gale.cengage.com

For product information and technology assistance, contact us at

Gale Customer Support, 1-800-877-4253
For permission to use material from this text or product, submit all requests online at www.cengage.com/permissions

Further permissions questions can be emailed to permissionrequest@cengage.com

Articles in Greenhaven Press anthologies are often edited for length to meet page requirements. In addition, original titles of these works are changed to clearly present the main thesis and to explicitly indicate the author's opinion. Every effort is made to ensure that Greenhaven Press accurately reflects the original intent of the authors. Every effort has been made to trace the owners of copyrighted material.

Cover image copyright © Images.com/Corbis.

LIBRARY OF CONGRESS CATALOGING-IN-PUBLICATION DATA

Designer babies / Clay Farris Naff, book editor.
    p. cm. -- (At Issue)
    Summary: "At Issue: Designer Babies: Books in this anthology series focus a wide range of viewpoints onto a single controversial issue, providing in-depth discussions by leading advocates, a quick grounding in the issues, and a challenge to critical thinking skills"-- Provided by publisher.
    Includes bibliographical references and index.
    ISBN 978-0-7377-6163-4 (hardback) -- ISBN 978-0-7377-6164-1 (paperback)
    1. Human reproductive technology. I. Naff, Clay Farris, editor of compilation.
    RG133.5.D468 2013
    616.6'9206--dc23
                                                    2012034056

Printed in the United States of America
1 2 3 4 5 6 7 16 15 14 13 12

Contents

Introduction

In his groundbreaking 1932 novel *Brave New World*, writer Aldous Huxley envisioned a future in which advances in fertility technology would eliminate natural reproduction in mankind. Instead, he imagined, embryos would be modified to predetermine intellect, physical prowess, and beauty. As a consequence, in his novel society becomes stratified into a rigid caste system. Now, less than a century later, developments in the science of genetics may be opening the door for science fiction to become reality. Within a few short years, some scientists claim, reproductive science could give birth to the age of "designer babies."

The term was coined to denote children whose genetic characteristics have been artificially selected or modified to ensure specific intellectual and cosmetic characteristics. Although both medical and legal obstacles remain in place, it is possible that soon parents could walk into a clinic and select not only their baby's gender, but also their height, hair, and eye color. As genetic science progresses, some expect that other characteristics, such as athletic or cognitive ability, will be enhanceable on demand.

The scenario of an artificially created race of genetically enhanced super-humans has brought forth comparisons between the designer baby of the future and the eugenics of Hitler's Third Reich.

Yet there are those, like transhumanist James Hughes, who see the genetic modification of humans as not only a natural progression of our species, but a right "in the same category as abortion." For Hughes, "if you think women have the right to control their bodies, then they should be able to make this choice."[1]

Despite the controversy, the actual science of designer babies is rooted in technology that is widely supported by the reproductive medical community and public. Pre-implantation genetic diagnosis, or PGD, is a fairly common procedure that allows doctors to screen embryos for the presence of genetic defects before they are implanted into a woman's uterus. Used in tandem with IVF or in vitro fertilization, PGD allows parents who are fearful of passing on devastating genetic diseases to their children some peace of mind. A couple with a family history of a genetic condition like Tay-Sach's disease or a chromosomal anomaly like Down syndrome, for example, can ensure that only healthy embryos are selected for implantation.

With such great potential for preventing life-threatening disease, it is not surprising that a majority of Americans support the use of PGD. However, when screening is opened up to include traits unrelated to health, 72% disapprove of the procedure, according to a June 2006 paper published by Kathy L. Hudson of the Genetics and Public Policy Center. Many, therefore, want the government to draw and enforce a line between acceptable and unacceptable uses for PGD. Reproductive science is moving faster than potential regulation, however, and the list of genetic characteristics under consideration is lengthening.

Sharon Duchesneau and her partner Candy McCullough have both been deaf since birth and view the condition as a positive and defining characteristic of their family rather than a disability. When the two decided to become mothers, Duchesneau and McCullough approached several sperm banks, requesting a donor who was also congenitally deaf. After being turned away by several clinics, the couple connected with a friend who had a long family history of deafness who agreed to donate his sperm.

Gauvin, who was carried by Duchesneau, was born nearly deaf, with limited hearing in one ear. When the story reached the media, many were outraged, believing that Duchesneau and McCullough had intentionally handicapped their son. Despite the very public backlash, the couple insisted, as Duchesneau wrote on her website, that "with an enhanced sense of smell, touch, and sight, Gauvin is not disabled, he is blessed."[2]

As genetic and reproductive science march steadily forward, private fertility clinics are also pushing the boundaries. In 2009, the Fertility Institutes in Los Angeles offered to let parents select their children's hair and eye color. Given that the fertility industry brings in $4 billion a year, it is easy to see why the Institutes' Jeff Steinberg would be eager for his clinic to be the pioneer of human genetic modification in America.

The reaction of the public, however, was swift and decidedly negative. The day after proclaiming the Fertility Institutes' doors open to parents seeking their very own designer baby, the clinic changed its policy. In a statement released to the media, the clinic declared that "Though well intended, we remain sensitive to public perception and feel that any benefit the diagnostic studies may offer are far outweighed by the apparent negative societal impacts involved."[3]

And so, the age of the designer baby is yet one of the future. What remains unclear is just how near or far that future looms. While PGD is still only used in the United States for medical purposes, breakthroughs connecting our knowledge of genes and the cosmetic traits they create come with ever-increasing frequency. The science of genetics is not waiting, and most analysts say that this technology cannot long be restricted from use by the public. At most, it can be regulated. *At Issue: Designer Babies* explores the ethical, moral, and medical implications of this technology as well as whether and how it should be regulated.

Notes

1. Quoted in Brandon Keim, "Designer Babies: A Right to Choose?" *Wired*, March 9, 2009. http://www.wired.com/wiredscience/2009/03/designerdebate/.

2. Quoted in Daniel Jeffreys, "Born to Be Deaf," *Daily Mail* Online, accessed April 24, 2012, http://www.dailymail.co.uk /health/article-108540/Born-deaf.html.
3. Quoted in Babylifestyles.com, "Designer Baby Plan Put on Hold at LA Fertility Clinic," March 6, 2009. http://www .babylifestyles.com/2009/03/designer-baby-plan-put-on -hold-at-la-fertility-clinic/.

1

A Big Step Toward "Designer Babies"—and Big Questions

Christian Science Monitor

The Christian Science Monitor *is an international news organization that delivers global coverage via its website and weekly magazine.*

Recent technology has allowed scientists to be able to map the DNA of a fetus. This new technology might allow parents to prenatally change disease-causing genes or even pick certain characteristics they would like their child to have. This potential for "designer babies" poses many ethical and legal questions. Although there is valid concern for abuse of this technology, it could also eliminate certain diseases and better human lives.

A stunning breakthrough in biotechnology was announced this week that brings humanity closer to an Orwellian prospect: parents being able to choose the characteristics of an unborn child.

For the first time, scientists have mapped the DNA of a fetus. They did so by using specimens from a pregnant woman and the father. The procedure may make it easier someday to prenatally change genes seen as causing diseases or, more startling, pick a child's attributes such as eye color or even intelligence.

This achievement by researchers at the University of Washington raises anew many legal, ethical, and moral concerns about the potential for "designer babies." Yet at a deeper level, such advances in the human mastery of the reproductive process also stir up questions about what is "natural"—or rather, whether "natural selection" will, or should, become "deliberate selection."

The power to alter a child's genetic makeup should not be regarded as simply an exercise in manipulating matter for a determined end. Rather it must also force fresh thinking about the principles that drive human behavior, such as the love that motivates a parent to be a parent or the truth about life's eternal nature that demands more than a desire for physical perfection in a child.

The technique of altering a fetus's DNA could simply push parents to treat children as a commodity, like a perfect Build-A-Bear, rather than treat them as a gift—one that commands unceasing love regardless of how a child turns out. But faced with the prospect of wielding immense control over a child's future, parents could also be humbled at the responsibility, even frightened at having to make so many choices that are now beyond the power of humans.

The technique of altering a fetus's DNA could simply push parents to treat children as a commodity, like a perfect Build-A-Bear, rather than treat them as a gift . . .

This is why critics call these techniques "playing God." Or as bioethicist Leon Kass has put it: "It's an ancient tension between, on the one hand, wanting to savor the world as it is and, on the other hand, wanting to improve on the world as given. There is a danger that the freedom to transform everything embraces the freedom to transform our own nature and even to destroy that very freedom itself."

Each new biotech advance in reproduction could help enlighten humans about their grander life purpose. When famed biologist J. Craig Venter became the first person to discover the sequence of the human genome in 2000, he said his work was inspired by the knowledge that "the human spirit is at least as important as our physiology."

"We're clearly much, much more than the sum total of our genes, just as our society is greater than the sum total of each of us," he stated.

The science of DNA is moving far faster than the human capacity to fully grasp its meaning. Even the researchers of this latest technique acknowledge in their paper that "our capacity to generate data is outstripping our ability to interpret it."

Such research is a double-edged sword. There is valid concern about the potential for abuse. But it can also be a window into higher concepts of humanity.

Before this kind of scientific work gets too far ahead, parallel research is needed in the ethics and morality of such advances. Tellingly, that desire for understanding can't be found in any gene.

2

Claims of an Age of Designer Babies Are Exaggerated

Mike Celizic

Mike Celizic is a columnist, writer, and author who is a regular online contributor to MSNBC.com, NBCSports.com and the To-day Show. The New Jersey–based journalist was previously managing editor of Strauss Newspapers.

The announcement by a clinic that specializes in sex selection that it is moving into "designer baby" services has prompted a lot of speculation about just how extensive such services might be. Some have wondered if such clinics could give parents the opportunity to pick their child's traits like items off a menu. Highly unlikely, say the experts. The announcement is more hype than reality. Although the clinic claims a 100 percent success rate in sex selection, this does not translate to similar success for particular genetic traits. Even the clinic admits it can only boost the chances that a baby's eye color will be what the parents request—and at a cost of around $18,000 per attempt. As for more complicated traits, such as intelligence or athletic ability, the experts scoff at the notion that these can be selected.

Imagine ordering a baby like dinner: "We'll take the boy in the Greek-god model, but can you make him 6-foot-4 instead of 6 feet? And gimme the green eyes instead of the blue; ash-blond hair—a little curly, but not too much; olive complexion; 140 IQ; heavy on the fast-twitch muscles."

Sound like science fiction? Maybe not: The news that a California fertility clinic is offering prospective parents the opportunity to improve the odds of having children with preselected hair, skin and eye color has renewed the debate over "designer babies." But Dr. Jamie Grifo, director of the Division of Reproductive Endocrinology at the NYU School of Medicine, told *Today*'s Meredith Vieira Tuesday [March 3, 2009] in New York that the issue is overblown. "I think this is more hype than reality," Grifo said.

A Costly and Chancy Procedure

Grifo is a pioneer in a technique called preimplantation genetic diagnosis (PGD) that has been widely used to screen for genetic diseases for 17 years. The procedure involves taking a cell from an embryo a few days after fertilization and scanning the DNA for certain diseases, such as Tay-Sachs, Down syndrome and a predisposition for certain types of cancer. It can also be used to select the gender of a baby.

> *Surveys ... show a high percentage of parents who would screen for mental retardation or genetic diseases, but few who want to determine physical appearance.*

The California clinic is using the same technique to increase the chances of having a baby with a specified eye, hair or skin color. Grifo said that surveys conducted by NYU show a high percentage of parents who would screen for mental retardation or genetic diseases, but few who want to determine physical appearance.

"Demand for that is not that high. Patients don't do it when they find out what's involved," he told Vieira. "You have to go through IVF. It costs a lot of money. It doesn't always work."

Published reports put the cost of selecting for the likelihood of physical traits at $18,000, and because it has to be done through in vitro fertilization, the procedure often has to be repeated multiple times before a viable fetus develops.

Trait-Picking Raises Concerns

The ability to choose a higher likelihood of certain physical traits is being advertised by the Fertility Institutes, a California fertility clinic headed by Dr. Jeffrey Steinberg, who was on the team of doctors that created the first so-called test-tube baby in the 1970s. Steinberg's clinic claims a 100 percent success rate over the years in selecting the gender of nearly 1,000 babies.

But Steinberg doesn't promise certainty with other traits, just an increased probability. "Can they say to me, 'We would prefer to have blue eyes,' and can we offer them an increased chance of blue eyes? Absolutely. Can we prefer curly hair? Absolutely," he told NBC News.

The 1997 film "Gattaca" portrayed a world in which parents select all the traits of their children. That vision scares many lay people as well as medical ethicists.

Marcy Darnovsky of the Center for Genetics and Society told NBC News that she fears Steinberg's clinic is starting society "down a slippery slope ... We do need some rules of the road. What kind of society are we working toward? I think we want to get away from prejudices based on the way people look."

Grifo agreed that selecting for appearance is not a good idea. "I don't think this is what we should be doing," he said. "I don't think patients really want this."

Complex Traits Elude Science

He also said that being able to select for such traits as intelligence and athletic ability is far in the future, because those traits involve combinations of genes as well as other factors.

"The science is kind of there," Grifo told Vieira. "You can pick the possibility that you have a higher chance of having a blue-eyed, blond-haired baby. But things like intelligence, sports [and] athletic ability, those genes we don't know. We don't know how to select for them, and I don't think we'll be able to select for them."

He also pointed out that when his group did the first PGD procedure in the 1990s, critics began warning about designer babies. "In 17 years, it hasn't happened. Yes, there is some gender selection going on. Most clinics will only do that for couples who want to balance their family; they have two girls, they want a boy," he said.

You can pick the possibility that you have a higher chance of having a blue-eyed, blond-haired baby. But things like intelligence, sports [and] athletic ability, those genes we don't know.

Focus on Healthy Babies

NYU's surveys have convinced him there simply isn't a great demand for the services Steinberg is offering.

"Who wants this?" Grifo asked. "I don't want this for my child. Patients tell me that. I don't think there's going to be a lot of people running to do this."

Still, if it becomes a problem, Grifo added, "I think people can stop it." But he said that would be a decision for lawmakers.

Grifo also cautioned that the hype over Steinberg's claims should not obscure the suffering and pain that PGD has helped to eliminate for thousands of parents.

"Imagine having a child die of a serious illness . . . and then knowing that you have a 25 to 50 percent risk of having another baby with that serious illness," Grifo told Vieira. "If you're that couple, you want this technology. You want to have a healthy baby. You don't want to experience that again. This technology allows these couples to have a healthy baby. That's a great thing."

He concluded: "It would be a shame for these people to be left out because of the trivial use of the technology."

3

The Nonmedical Screening of Embryos Should Be Banned

Cheryl Miller

Cheryl Miller is editor of Doublethink, *a publication of the conservative America's Future Foundation. She is a 2007 Phillips Foundation Journalism Fellow, writing on assisted reproductive technology and the American family. Previously, she was assistant to columnist David Brooks at the* New York Times, *deputy director of research at the White House Office of Speechwriting, and associate editor of* The New Atlantis.

Dr. Jeffrey Steinberg's announcement about plans to offer trait selection services at his clinic is symptomatic of the unregulated market for assisted reproduction services in the United States. In contrast to most other advanced nations, the United States has not passed laws to limit the nonmedical use of preimplantation embryo screening. Although Steinberg's clinic is only offering simple trait-selection techniques, far more extensive uses of trait selection are bound to follow, unless preventive legislative action is taken. The combination of profit opportunity and parents' bottomless desire to give their children advantages will assure that the technology advances. Most Americans are against an unregulated market for such services. Their wishes should be enacted into laws.

You may think Dr. Jeff Steinberg, who made headlines last week [March 2009] for offering to customize babies' hair and eye color, is an anomaly. But get ready for more doctors just like him. The age of designer babies—with all the troubling moral implications that idea carries—is here, unless we pass strong laws to fend it off, as other nations have done.

The United States has long been regarded as the Wild West of assisted reproduction. The $3 billion fertility industry operates with virtually no rules or regulatory oversight.

This is in stark contrast to the rest of the developed world, where the majority of countries have a national regulatory body policing fertility clinics. Indeed, of the 30 industrialized countries—which account for one-fifth of the world's population and have the most fully developed biotechnology sectors—77% have banned embryo screening for nonmedical purposes.

As technology marches on and the fairly crude trait-selection tools that Steinberg said he would employ give way to much more sophisticated methods, the U.S. seems determined to keep its head in the sand. While the American Society for Reproductive Medicine [ASRM] provides guidelines, they are purely voluntary and the society rarely sanctions a clinic for a violation.

In fact, a 2006 Centers for Disease Control and Prevention report found that fewer than 20% of the nation's clinics abided by the ASRM's rules regarding how many embryos should be transferred. Unsurprisingly, Fertility Institutes, where Steinberg works, is among the clinics in violation of this guideline.

One Small Step

Yes, it's true. Steinberg has, for now, put his eye-color and hair-color trait-selection business on the back burner—saying he will only offer similar services to couples seeking to prevent genetic defects. And other fertility doctors insist that the science Steinberg boasted about simply doesn't allow the "designer baby" fear to play out in the real world.

Don't believe it. The science is advancing rapidly, doctors want to make money and for many parents the disturbing desire to tailor their future children is insatiable. The history of embryo screening makes clear: Once you start testing for some genes, it's tempting to start testing for others.

Initially, embryo screening targeted only severe abnormalities like Tay-Sachs. Since then, we've started screening for many more, less serious defects, including diseases with late-adult onset, manageable conditions—like arthritis—and even easily treatable defects like a cleft palate.

The leap from preventing birth defects to ordering up a perfectly healthy, attractive child is actually, at this point, a very small jump. This should trouble everyone who believes in the dignity, uniqueness and value of every human life.

Sex selection—originally intended to prevent sex-linked diseases—is now available to anyone who wants to arrange their family just so. Want your first child to be a boy? There are now hundreds of clinics that will be happy to oblige you.

And so, the leap from preventing birth defects to ordering up a perfectly healthy, attractive child is actually, at this point, a very small jump. This should trouble everyone who believes in the dignity, uniqueness and value of every human life.

Heading Off Future Dangers

Even though the U.S. is the Wild West, there's one Western country we should consider a cautionary tale: the United Kingdom. There, doctors claim cosmetic selection of embryos is necessary to protect against "family distress." One physician even weeded out embryos for a couple who wanted to avoid a congenital squint.

Screening for cosmetic traits is only the tip of the iceberg. In the not-so-distant future, we'll have to contend with ever more difficult dilemmas: Should we select for social traits like intelligence? We now allow deaf parents to select for deaf offspring—will we allow straight parents to select for straight children, and gay parents for gay children?

And when these possibilities become realities, will we see the rich taking advantage of them, leaving the un-enhanced poor on the outside looking in?

We can't tiptoe around these questions any longer. It's time to tame the Wild West. A majority of Americans want more oversight of reproductive technologies, and—as the outcry over Steinberg's clinic shows—disapprove of screening for cosmetic traits.

We have consensus. So what are we waiting for?

4

Designer Baby Technologies Cannot Be Stopped by Bans

William Saletan

William Saletan is a correspondent for the online magazine Slate. *He frequently writes about controversial topics in his column "Human Nature." A native of Texas, Saletan graduated from Swarthmore College in suburban Philadelphia.*

The effort to draw a clear line between therapeutic and aesthetic uses of "designer baby" technology is doomed. Too many converging trends favor the nearly seamless move from selecting against embryos that have fatal genetic flaws to selecting for embryos that carry favored traits, such as preferred hair or eye color. Among the trends: half the clinics in the United States that offer screening allow sex selection along with genetic disease detection; the technology for trait selection is improving; and the market for such services has become global. Bans in one country will only shift the demand to another.

Is the era of designer babies finally here?

Every week, it seems, we're told that this discovery or that technology might lead to "designer babies." I've heard this so many times that I've stopped taking it seriously. Genetic engineering always turns out to be more complicated than expected, and our latest technology always turns out to be less capable than advertised.

But now trait selection seems to be coming into view for real.

Two months ago [in December, 2008], the Fertility Institutes, an assisted reproduction company headquartered in Los Angeles, began advertising the "pending availability" of genetic tests that would offer "a preselected choice of gender, eye color, hair color and complexion" in artificially conceived children. On Thursday [February 13, 2009], Gautam Naik of the *Wall Street Journal* reported that "half a dozen" potential clients had contacted the company to request such tests. As of today [February 17, 2009], the tests still aren't for sale. But several trends are converging to make aesthetic trait selection an impending business.

[T]ens of thousands of embryos have been screened for quality and potential disease. . . . Culturally and politically, there's no going back.

Trends Point the Same Way

1. *Embryo screening has become permanently entrenched.* By now, tens of thousands of embryos have been screened for quality and potential disease, thanks to preimplantation genetic diagnosis [PGD]. Culturally and politically, there's no going back.

2. *Screening is steadily expanding to traits that are less medically important.* We're examining and discarding embryos for flaws that are less lethal, less harmful, less likely to cause disease, and less likely to strike early in life. Two years ago [in 2007] British regulators approved PGD to get rid of embryos that might become grotesquely cross-eyed. At the time, the head of the clinic that pioneered this use of PGD predicted, "We will increasingly see the use of embryo screening for severe cosmetic conditions."

3. *Aesthetic screening is spreading.* Once you're screening for "severe" cosmetic conditions, you can no longer rule out other cosmetic criteria. The principal gateway to aesthetic use of PGD is sex selection. Worldwide, the number of embryos and fetuses discarded for being the wrong sex is in the millions. In this country, the number of clients paying for sex-selective PGD is in the thousands and growing. Nearly half of U.S. clinics that offer PGD have used it for nonmedical sex selection, and 40 percent of Americans approve of this practice. The Fertility Institutes explicitly frames eye, hair, and skin color selection as an extension of sex selection.

4. *A market for nonmedical trait selection is emerging.* Naik points to a New York University survey of patients seeking genetic counseling. In the survey, published three weeks ago, 10 to 13 percent of respondents said they would use PGD to select height, athletic ability, or intelligence. NYU spins this as a tiny minority. But in raw numbers, it's easily enough to attract opportunistic entrepreneurs.

5. *Aesthetic trait selection is becoming feasible.* This used to be the sticking point in bringing the technology to market. No more. Naik reports:

> In October 2007, scientists from deCode Genetics of Iceland published a paper in *Nature Genetics* pinpointing various [genes] that influence skin, eye and hair color, based on samples taken from people in Iceland and the Netherlands. Along with related genes discovered earlier, "the variants described in this report enable prediction of pigmentation traits based upon an individual's DNA," the company said. . . . William Kearns, a medical geneticist and director of the Shady Grove Center for Preimplantation Genetics in Rockville, Md., says he has made headway in cracking the problem. In a presentation made at a November meeting of the American Society of Human Genetics in Philadelphia, he described how he had managed to amplify the DNA available from a single embryonic cell to identify complex diseases and also certain physical traits. Of 42 embryos

tested, Dr. Kearns said he had enough data to identify [genes] that relate to northern European skin, hair and eye pigmentation in 80% of the samples.

Kearns isn't offering his method for aesthetic PGD. He adamantly opposes this application as an unethical abuse of the technology. But his breakthrough inadvertently shows less scrupulous followers how they could serve their own ends. Dr. Kearns says he is firmly against the idea of using PGD to select nonmedical traits. He plans to offer his PGD amplification technique to fertility clinics for medical purposes such as screening for complex disorders, but won't let it be used for physical trait selection. "I'm not going to do designer babies," says Dr. Kearns. "I won't sell my soul for a dollar."

6. *Doctors have an easy way to talk themselves into offering the service.* Dr. Jeffrey Steinberg, medical director of the Fertility Institutes, sees trait selection as a natural extension of the road his profession is already traveling. "This is cosmetic medicine," he tells the *Journal*. Watch Steinberg's promotional video, and you'll see how easy it is to sell trait selection as just another consumer service. Reproductive technology can "help fertile and infertile couples choose the gender they've always wished for," the video's female narrator promises. Steinberg appears on camera, assuring potential customers that his personnel are experts at "evaluating embryos and making sure that people get their request for a boy or a girl." You want a girl? We'll get you a girl. You want a blonde? We'll get you a blonde.

7. *Patients have an easy way to talk themselves into buying the service.* You don't have to request PGD just to screen your embryos for eye or hair color. That might feel icky. Instead, Steinberg offers you a package deal:

> Patients having genetic screening for abnormal chromosome conditions in their embryos will be able to elect expanded testing that can greatly increase the odds of achieving a healthy pregnancy with a preselected choice of gender, eye

color, hair color and complexion, along with screening for potentially lethal diseases, screening for cancer tendencies (breast, colon, pancreas, prostate) and more.

See how smooth the transition can be? You're already screening for diseases. Why not add one more factor while you're at it? So now you'll know which embryos are male and which are female, just in case two of them turn out to be healthy and you're lucky enough to be able to choose which one to put in the womb. And if you're checking sex, why not throw in eye color and complexion? You don't have to do anything with the information yet. Just run the test and find out what your options are.

8. *Globalization thwarts regulation.* "A large majority of industrialized countries—including Canada, the UK, most of Europe, Japan, Israel, China, and Australia—prohibits nonmedical sex selection," notes the Center for Genetics and Society. But the United States doesn't, and according to CGS Associate Director Marcy Darnovsky, Steinberg exploits this gap by "offering travel packages so that people can come to the US to dodge laws in their home nations." CGS wants tougher U.S. laws. Good luck with that: Steinberg already has a satellite clinic in Mexico.

This is how revolutions happen: Technology matures, trends converge, and cultural changes pave the way. By the time Steinberg opens his trait-selection business and does for that practice what he's already doing for sex selection, it'll be too late to stop him. In fact, before you know it, we'll be used to it.

5

Expert Opinions Should Guide Designer Baby Technologies

Sirine Shebaya

Sirine Shebaya is a philosopher who focuses on bioethics and healthcare issues at the Johns Hopkins Berman Institute of Bioethics. She earned her doctorate in philosophy at Columbia University and served as the Greenwall Fellow in Bioethics and Health Policy from 2007 to 2009.

Scientific advances in human development attract a lot of media attention and raise concerns about the prospect of designer babies. This response was especially notable after scientists employed genetic engineering to create a human embryo from scratch. The embryo was quickly destroyed, but the fears linger on. Such a technological capacity holds great potential for alleviating genetic diseases, but also for misuse. Therefore, a broad public discussion is appropriate. The potential for misuse alone cannot, by itself, be the basis for a decision to ban the technology outright. Slippery slope arguments—the idea that if you allow one marginal practice, it will inevitably lead to an array of reprehensible practices—are also not valid justifications for bans. Instead, public discussion should lead to selective bans on misuses and regulation of beneficial uses.

The media is abuzz with news of researchers at Cornell University successfully creating the first genetically engineered human embryo. The embryo was destroyed after five days, but critics argue that this is a first step towards "designer babies," and that the scientists overstepped by making a decision on a controversial subject without consulting the public or opening the issue up for an informed discussion. In order to properly weigh the ethical issues, one relevant piece of information we must consider is the goal of the experiment and its projected benefits. The potential rewards of this work are immense, but we should not scoff at the possibility that this kind of research could ultimately lead to the technology for creating babies with preselected mental or physical traits.

The scientists argue that the embryo they used was not viable—it had three sets of chromosomes rather than the normal two—and therefore could not have developed into a baby anyway. They also claim that since the research, focused on stem cells, was privately funded and passed their internal review board, they violated no federal regulations. The suggestion was even made that this did not constitute a huge technological advance because the technique is already commonly used for gene therapy. So was there anything ethically irresponsible about their experiment? And what can we conclude about this type of research in general?

Great Potential

The scientists claim that their goal was to find out if genetic changes made to embryos can be passed on to daughter cells. Genetic modifications in an embryo are thought to be inheritable, whereas current gene therapy—genetic modification performed on people for disease treatment purposes—cannot be passed on to future generations. The potential benefits of heritable genetic modification are huge—for instance, individuals could potentially rid their offspring of a gene that would predispose them to breast cancer—but so are its potential abuses. We cannot assume without discussion that preselecting our offspring's genetic makeup is not an undesirable outcome.

Scientists constantly emphasize that we are still a long way away from children with preselected traits. But declining to regulate research that could lead us to a point where such choices are possible is troubling precisely because we cannot expect individual scientists to censor themselves based on a concern for societal consequences. This is arguably not their job. Remember division of labor and how it increases efficiency? Scientists have a mission to explore and pursue the most promising avenues of research within the bounds of government regulations. Policy makers and legislators have a mission to figure out where the lines ought to be drawn. Whether we like the idea of "designer babies" or not, their possibility would entail quite serious public and societal consequences. Decisions about the issue have to be made not simply at the level of individual scientists and research labs, but at the public, societal level, particularly given the extent of moral disagreements on the matter.

The mere fact that a particular type of research could lead to undesirable applications is not a good reason to ban the research if it also has sufficiently important good consequences. Instead, it is a good reason to ban the undesirable applications.

As members of a recent AAAS [American Association for the Advancement of Science] panel on stem cell research have pointed out, the mere existence of moral controversy is not in itself sufficient to determine the ethical standing of an experiment or research direction. However, the existence of moral controversy mandates a public ethical review and a set of regulations consistent both with expert opinions and with social values.

Worries Don't Warrant Ban

Slippery slope worries can be compelling in some cases, but not everything is a slippery slope. The mere fact that a particular type of research *could* lead to undesirable applications is not a good reason to ban the research if it also has sufficiently important good consequences. Instead, it is a good reason to ban the undesirable applications. The best way to avoid slippery slopes to bad outcomes is to have an informed, democratic discussion that takes into account both expert opinions and social values. We need regulations because scientists and the general public need clarity about what they can and cannot do, a convincing rationale for permissions and restrictions, and a voice in arriving at decisions with such important ramifications.

6

The Need to Regulate "Designer Babies"

Scientific American

Scientific American, founded in 1845, is a print and online magazine that focuses on science, technology, and policy.

Preimplantation genetic diagnosis, or PGD, is a technique that allows the screening of embryos before they are implanted in the womb. While initial procedures focused on aiding parents in avoiding passing on devastating genetic diseases, limited governmental regulation has led to the expansion of the traits being screened. The Fertility Institutes pulled the plug on its initial plans to use PGD to offer parents the ability to choose their future baby's hair, eye, and skin color following strong negative reactions from the public as well as widespread media attention. Without government restriction, however, the Institutes are unlikely to entirely abandon their attempts to make embryonic selection available to the general public, and there is little stopping other private clinics from doing the same. Given the complexity of regulating PGD, the United States should look to Britain, which already has in place a functioning set of laws limiting reproductive technologies. The system can provide a legal guideline for the United States to develop its own regulations.

*M*ore oversight is needed to prevent misuse of new reproductive technologies.

On March 3 the cover story of the *New York Daily News* trumpeted a simple imperative to "Design Your Baby." The screaming headline related to a service that would try to allow parents to choose their baby's hair, eye and skin color. A day later the Fertility Institutes reconsidered. The organization made an "internal, self regulatory decision" to scrap the project because of "public perception" and the "apparent negative societal impacts involved," it noted in a statement.

The change of heart will do nothing to stymie the dawning era of what the article called "Build-A-Bear" babies. The use (and abuse) of advanced fertility technology that evokes fears of *Gattaca, Brave New World* and, of course, the Nazis' quest for a blonde, blue-eyed race of Aryans continues apace. A recent survey found that about 10 percent of a group who went for genetic counseling in New York City expressed interest in screening for tall stature and that some 13 percent said they would be willing to test for superior intelligence. The Fertility Institutes is still building the foundation for a nascent dial-a-trait catalogue: it routinely accepts clients who wish to select the sex of their child.

The decision to scrap the designer baby service came just a few weeks after Nadya Suleman, a single, unemployed California mother living on food stamps, gained notoriety after giving birth to octuplets through in vitro fertilization. The Suleman brouhaha showed that even routine uses of reproductive technologies can be fraught with issues that bear on ethics and patient safety.

The preimplantation genetic diagnosis (PGD) technique used by the Fertility Institutes to test embryos before implantation in the womb has enabled thousands of parents to avoid passing on serious genetic diseases to their offspring. Yet fertility specialists are doing more than tiptoeing into a new era in which medical necessity is not the only impetus for seeking help. In the U.S., no binding rules deter a private clinic from offering a menu of traits or from implanting a woman with a collection of embryos. Physicians who may receive more than $10,000 for a procedure serve as the sole arbiters of a series of thorny ethical, safety and social welfare questions. The 33-year-old Suleman already had six children, and her physician implanted her with six embryos, two of which split into twins. American Society for Reproductive Medicine (ASRM) voluntary guidelines suggest that, under normal circumstances, no more than two embryos be transferred to a woman younger than 35 because of the risk of complications.

> *The intricacies of regulating fertility technology requires more careful consideration that can only come with a measure of federal guidance. As part of the push toward health care reform, the Obama administration should carefully inspect the British model.*

Of course, any office consultation with a fertility doctor will likely neglect the nuances of more encompassing ethical dilemmas. Should parents be allowed to pick embryos for specific tissue types so that their new baby can serve as a donor for an ailing sibling? For that matter, should a deaf parent who embraces his or her condition be permitted to select an embryo apt to produce a child unable to hear? Finally, will selection of traits perceived to be desirable end up diminishing variability within the gene pool, the raw material of natural selection?

In the wake of the octuplets' birth, some legislators made hasty bids to enact regulation at the state level—and one bill was drafted with the help of antiabortion advocates. The intricacies of regulating fertility technology requires more careful consideration that can only come with a measure of federal guidance. As part of the push toward health care reform, the Obama administration should carefully inspect the British model.

Since 1991 the U.K.'s Human Fertilization and Embryology Authority (HFEA) has made rules for in vitro fertilization and any type of embryo manipulation. The HFEA licenses clinics and regulates research: it limits the number of embryos implanted and prohibits sex selection for nonmedical reasons, but it is not always overly restrictive. It did not object to using PGD to pick an embryo that led to the birth of a girl in January who lacked the genes that would have predisposed her to breast cancer later in life.

HFEA may not serve as a precise template for a U.S. regulatory body. But a close look at nearly two decades of licensing a set of reproductive technologies by the country that brought us the first test-tube baby may build a better framework than reliance on the good faith of physicians who confront an inherent conflict of interest.

7

Parents Should Be Free to Choose Their Babies' Characteristics

James Hughes, interviewed by Brandon Keim

James Hughes is a sociologist and bioethicist teaching health policy at Trinity College in Hartford, Connecticut. He also serves as executive director of the Institute for Ethics and Emerging Technologies. Brandon Keim is a science journalist. His work has been published in USA Today, Psychology Today, *and* Nature Medicine. *He has been featured on NPR, the BBC, and Animal Planet.*

According to bioethicist James Hughes, the uproar over a fertility clinic's offer to help parents select some of their offspring's traits is misplaced. Parents make choices for their children throughout their lives, so why shouldn't they make choices before a child is born? The kinds of choices the clinic is offering—hair or eye color—are harmless. Just as important, making such choices is part of the liberty parents should enjoy in raising their children. Of course, harmful choices should be distinguished and banned, just as child abuse is outlawed, but to assume that parents do not have their children's best interests in mind is insulting.

When a Los Angeles fertility clinic offered last month [February 2009] to let parents choose their kids' hair and eye color, public outrage followed. On March 2 [2009], the clinic shut the program down—and that, says transhumanist author James Hughes, is a shame.

According to Hughes, using reproductive technologies—in this case, pre-implantation genetic diagnosis (PGD), in which doctors screen embryos before implanting them—for cosmetic purposes is just an old-fashioned parental impulse, translated into 21st century technology. If nobody gets hurt and everybody has access, says Hughes, then genetic modification is perfectly fine, and restricting it is an assault on reproductive freedom. "It's in the same category as abortion. If you think women have the right to control their own bodies, then they should be able to make this choice," he said. "There should be no law restricting the kind of kids people have, unless there's gross evidence that they're going to harm that kid, or harm society." Hughes' views are hardly universal. "I'm totally against this," said William Kearns, the medical geneticist who developed the techniques used by the Fertility Institutes for cosmetic purposes, in a newspaper interview. In the same article, Mark Hughes, one of the inventors of pre-implantation genetic diagnosis, called its non-therapeutic use "ridiculous and irresponsible." Wired.com talked to James Hughes . . . about generic selection.

There should be no law restricting the kind of kids people have, unless there's gross evidence that they're going to harm that kid, or harm society.

An Expansion of Choice

Wired.com: What do you think about using reproductive technologies to pick cosmetic traits?

James Hughes: It's inevitable, in the broad context of freedom and choice. And the term "designer babies" is an insult to parents, because it basically says parents don't have their kids' best interests at heart.

The only people who are consistent about this are the Catholics.

They say that you have to accept whatever pops out of your procreative unions. But if you think that people have a right to choose how many children they have, or the partners they have them with—"I love you, but you're just too short, or too ugly"—that's a procreative choice.

If I've got a dozen embryos I could implant, and the ones I want to implant are the green-eyed ones, or the blond-haired ones, that's an extension of choices we think are perfectly acceptable—and restricting them [is] a violation of our procreative autonomy.

I want to see a society in which parents can say, I want my kids to have the best possible options in life. That might include getting rid of obesity genes. Every child should be a loved child, but there is no virtue in accident.

But one could argue that obesity is a health problem, not a cosmetic issue.

So parents are only allowed to have preferences about health conditions? What if we discovered that eating fish oil while pregnant increases intelligence, which it does? We're not going to say that you can't make certain dietary choices. In fact, we encourage them. And would we say it was morally inappropriate for parents to stand on their head during copulation, if it made their children blond? I doubt it. The only reason this is different is because it involves embryo selection.

But isn't this going to produce a super-race of children born to people wealthy enough to afford artificial reproduction?

Procreative Autonomy Is Paramount

Insofar as the choices are eye color and hair color, that's not going to exacerbate inequalities in society. It's a minor way in which greater wealth allows more reproductive choice, but it shouldn't be a reason to override reproductive freedom.

If PGD had the ability to double the IQs of children— which it doesn't—then that would be the sort of inequality that warranted a social policy against it. I'm worried about that situation, not hair and eye color.

Gross exacerbation of social inequality is a grave social harm. That's why we need universal health care, and universal access to any technology which provides profound enablement.

It's hard to imagine these ever being universally available.

Medicaid has considered the provision of fertility services.

Some say fertility isn't a health issue—but I think that's B.S. Having a saline breast implant put in after a mastectomy isn't a health issue, but we pay for it, because it improves quality of life.

Some ethicists say that non-therapeutic reproductive technologies shouldn't be used until the industry is better-regulated.

Fertility clinics and reproductive medicine need a complete revamping of their regulatory structures. Many of the procedures are not being monitored for safety and efficacy. But those are the only two grounds on which to base a legitimate socictal regulation.

Where do you draw the line? What if I want disabled children?

We've been debating that for five or six years, ever since a deaf lesbian couple in Chicago wanted to use PGD to choose among the embryos they'd fertilized for one that inherited a form of deafness.

The reproductive autonomy of parents should be protected at a high level—and that even includes decisions that impose a degree of harm on children.

They said that deafness is a perfectly benign condition, and that living in the hearing world is like living in the white world as a black person.

I argue in *Citizen Cyborg* that I wouldn't want to see a law saying you can't do this, but I'd want to see strong moral sanctions.

The reproductive autonomy of parents should be protected at a high level—and that even includes decisions that impose a degree of harm on children.

But what if I wanted to have a child who was deformed?

I think a principle developed by Peter Singer is useful: If you think parents should be punished for taking that ability away from a child who's already born, that's probably harm.

8

Enhancing Humans Through Science Is Beneficial

Hemmy Cho

Hemmy Cho is Global Programme Manager at Google. Previously, she worked as a multiplatform trainer and product manager at the BBC, specializing in TV, radio, web, gaming, and social media.

Out of the development of gene science has emerged a new relationship between humans and evolution. Rather than relying on natural selection, parents can now select certain traits for future children. While these advancements have stirred up controversy, designer babies are not the first or only example of humans enhancing their natural states through science. Technology is now moving beyond aids like artificial limbs, which are a substitute for a lost ability, and into giving people "superhuman" powers. Whether genetic selection or technological innovation, these movements in artificial human enhancement bring forward many ethical and societal questions, but all people should be able to benefit from important and worthwhile advancements in human technology.

I recently spent a day with married friends and their beautiful one-year-old girl, Lily. Lily smiled, giggled and ooh-ed at everything and everyone around her. She was simply delighted to be there, in that non-descript café-bar on the South Bank on a grey London afternoon. When she cracked one of those gorgeous sunny smiles at you, it wasn't for any other reason but because she was there, now and she was very pleased about it, and you couldn't help but feel pleased yourself.

Lily is the perfect baby. Cute, pretty, smiley, well-behaved, fun, smart. If people could choose to design their babies, they would make her like Lily. Currently, our knowledge of genetics is not enough to select much more than gender or eliminate certain diseases, but advances in genetics in the future will probably make it possible for parents to 'design' their babies while they are still embryos, i.e. select the gender, hair colour, personality, IQ, and eliminate any diseases and 'negative' traits such as anti-social tendencies. Would it be a problem for you if Lily, in all her perfection, had been genetically modified?

Beyond Evolution

[Ethologist] Richard Dawkins has suggested that through evolution, certain traits get more and more specialized, but not necessarily better. This is because natural selection relies on random mutations of genes that enhance certain traits and thus help that individual to reproduce and pass on his or her genes. Over millennia, those traits that are most helpful to the propagation of the species will become more widespread. But now, advances in genetics mean we don't have to rely on evolution. We can choose the genes that we wish to pass onto our immediate future generations and bypass the genetic lottery.

Understandably, many debates rage around the ethics of 'designer babies.' Does the foetus have the right to not be genetically modified, or do parents own the right to change its genetic code to have the kind of child they want? Would the 'advantages' the parents endow upon the foetus in fact stop the child from experiencing character-building trials and make the child feel superior to its non-genetically modified peers? What if the child could be genetically engineered to be modest and kind as well as superior in intelligence, appearance and ability?

Many people feel uncomfortable with 'playing God' or being able to change someone else's destiny. But don't parents shape the child mentally, emotionally and physically after birth anyway through upbringing and the environment they provide for the child? Also throughout history, humans have been selecting the traits that they want in their children by selecting their mates. Why not give the child a head start with a little help from available science?

One could argue that everything we do to develop ourselves is 'enhancement' of our natural state, whether it's learning an instrument, foreign language, or social skills. On the physical side, parents paying for orthodontics and even breast enhancements for their children are accepted by society, so why not enhance the more fundamental and arguably more important aspects of our children like intelligence or memory before birth? . . .

[T]hroughout history, humans have been selecting the traits that they want in their children by selecting their mates. Why not give the child a head start with a little help from available science?

Technology Already Enhances People

[M]any ordinary people out there have "superpowers" already thanks to mechanical or technological enhancements. They are real-life cyborgs, defined as a being with both biological and artificial (e.g. electronic, mechanical or robotic) parts. And what's more, with our growing reliance on technology, we all seem to be well on our way to becoming cyborgs. What kind of ethical dilemmas might this bring to our society?

Daniel Kish, a man who's been sightless since a year old, is still able to mountain bike and camp out in the wilderness alone. He uses echolocation, the technique that bats use to see in the dark, which involves him clicking his tongue and interpreting the sound of the returning echo to figure out his surroundings. Most people rely on sight to navigate but Daniel has learned to use echolocation to do most things that sighted people can do, and in certain instances, can "see" his surroundings much better than them. His dream is to help all sight-impaired people see the world as clearly as he does. He is developing canes for the blind that would create the same range of sonar waves that bats send out, and hearing enhancements that would enable those blind people to hear a wider range of sound waves that are returned so they could navigate accurately just like a bat does.

[D]on't people have the right to change their bodies whichever way they see fit . . . ?

Enhancements like these are going one step further than, say, artificial limbs in that instead of acting as a poor substitute for an ability a person has lost, they actually give "superhuman" powers that are not part of ordinary human biological make-up and allow the person to do things other humans cannot do. . . .

There are people who already advocate the development and use of technology to improve the human condition by eliminating aging and enhancing human intellectual, physical and psychological capabilities. This international intellectual and cultural movement is called Transhumanism (often abbreviated to H+ or h+). They predict that human beings may eventually be able to transform themselves into beings with such greatly expanded abilities as to merit the label "posthuman". . . .

Many of the ["designer baby"] arguments could apply to transhumanism. Many people feel uncomfortable with "playing God", and philosophically and culturally, many people place a moral value on being "natural." But don't people have the right to change their bodies whichever way they see fit, as long as it's not harmful to themselves or others?

9

The Public Should Oppose Designer Baby Technology

Rahul Thadani

Rahul Thadani has written extensively for Buzzle.com, covering topics ranging from sports to cutting-edge scientific discoveries, and from food to home tattoo removal.

While the public may have little insight into new developments on the frontier of designer babies, the issue is intensely debated within the scientific community. As possibilities within genetic modification science expand, a world in which children can be selected for appearance, intelligence, and health seems just around the corner. The impact on society is hard to predict, but several ethical questions immediately arise. The hefty cost of the procedure means that few families will have access to the procedures, creating a wide divide between the poor and the genetically altered wealthy. Genetic diversity will also be greatly reduced, leaving the human race susceptible to certain diseases. There may be additional unintended consequences for the modified children themselves. While the basic intentions of the science behind designer babies are good, the potential for ethical entanglements is great. Humanity would be better off not pursuing such technologies.

> Alpha children wear gray. They work much harder than we do, because they're so frightfully clever. I'm awfully glad I'm a Beta, because I don't work so hard. And then we are much

better than the Gammas and Deltas. Gammas are stupid. They all wear green, and Delta children wear khaki. Oh no, I don't want to play with Delta children. And Epsilons are still worse. They're too stupid to be able to read or write. Besides they wear black, which is a beastly color. I'm so glad I'm a Beta.

When Aldous Huxley coined this quote in 1932 in his novel *Brave New World*, he had no idea how intense the designer babies debate could become less than a century after. His book was a satirical look into a Utopian society, where people were segregated on the basis of genetic modifications that they were subjected to as embryos. The end result was a seriously disillusioned world where these modifications brought on a revival of the dark ages.

The designer babies debate today is something that the public eye has been shielded from, and for good measure. Companies like Google and Amazon have banned advertisements of gene modifications in many countries, since this is an issue that really splits opinion. It is in the confines of scientific labs and multinational companies' conference halls that this debate is slowly rising and threatening to boil over.

> *The designer babies debate is . . . about how we are learning to sidestep nature, and how this could crumble society as we know it today.*

Defining Designer Babies

Before we get into designer babies ethical issues, it is crucial to understand what this truly means. Picture a world where parents of a yet unborn child can modify his/her genes, and thus determine his/her physical appearance, cleverness and resistance to disease. It sounds like stuff that science fiction movies are made of, but we are fast approaching a day when this method will be guaranteed to work. What happens to the world after that, remains to be seen.

According to the *Oxford English Dictionary*, a designer baby is 'A baby whose genetic makeup has been artificially selected by genetic engineering combined with IVF (In Vitro Fertilization) to ensure the presence or absence of particular genes or characteristics.' The process involves fertilizing the egg by the sperm in a test tube outside the mother's womb, and altering the genes. Admittedly, the purpose is noble (to eradicate genetic disorders and diseases), but where will the human race really draw the line? Who is to stop affluent families (for this is an expensive procedure) from using these methods to change their child's eye color, or to make him a professional football player, or to make her slender and gorgeous? The designer babies debate is more about how we are learning to sidestep nature, and how this could crumble society as we know it today.

The process of selecting the traits and characteristics of children is also known as Pre-implementation Genetic Diagnosis (PGD), and here the embryo is checked for genetic deficiencies before it is returned to the mothers' womb. Suitable alterations can be made along the way, and the repercussions that this will have is open for debate.

The human race must stop trying to play God by messing with genetics and embryo alterations, and this is exactly what the designer babies debates are all about.

An Ugly Outlook

The designer babies ethical considerations come into play because of the effects this procedure will have. Families that can afford these alterations will be few, and this will only increase the disparity between the various social classes. This will ultimately result in a segregation between the superior 'modified' humans, and the pure but inferior ones. Sooner or later, this situation will turn ugly. Moreover, the diversity of the gene pool and human genetics will be affected, and this may even lead to a major percentage of the human race being wiped out completely by some major disease. All this is without even taking into consideration the effect this procedure will have on the child.

People involved in designer babies debates sometimes forget to think about the effects these alterations will have on the children. After all, if you are tweaking one gene here, then another gene somewhere else must be shifting to balance the event. This could ultimately lead to a situation where each child is programmed to do certain tasks, and is unable to do anything else, much in the way Mr. Huxley envisaged. Moreover, the freedom of the child to choose a profession of his choice in the future, will also be severely diminished. The ethical repercussions of this are not very pleasant. . . .

The human race must stop trying to play God by messing with genetics and embryo alterations, and this is exactly what the designer babies debates are all about. Though it is too late to eradicate these procedures entirely, we can still do our best to control the situation. The purpose may be noble (to eradicate genetic diseases), but in the wrong hands this knowledge could be devastating. And human beings do have a tendency to allow such knowledge to ultimately fall into the wrong hands.

10

From Regenerative Medicine to Human Design: What Are We Really Afraid Of?

Gregory Stock

Gregory Stock (www.gregorystock.net) is a biophysicist, biotech entrepreneur, and an author. He received a PhD from Johns Hopkins and an MBA from the Harvard Business School and served as founding director of the Program of Medicine, Technology, and Society at UCLA's School of Medicine. He co-founded and directed Signum Biosciences, which is developing therapeutics for Alzheimer's, and Ecoeos, which is developing a genetic test to gauge personal susceptibility to mercury toxicity. Stock has served on the editorial boards of the International Journal of Bioethics, *the* American Journal of Bioethics, *and the* Journal of Evolution and Technology.

While humankind is on the verge of immense advances in biotechnology, this frontier is not the first scientific challenge humanity has explored. Developments in molecular biology will have an enormous impact on humanity, but we should not respond to these advances with fear. Advances in biotechnology will extend human life, improve health care, and lead to new medicines. As we increase our understanding of human genetics, we can also look forward to significant expansion of preimplantation genetic diagnosis, or PGD, and to advances in human reproductive cloning.

Gregory Stock, "From Regenerative Medicine to Human Design: What Are We Really Afraid Of?," *DNA and Cell Biology*, vol. 22, no. 11, 2003, pp. 679–683. http://www.siumed.edu/medhum/electives/HealthPolicyMedia/wk5Stock.pdf. Copyright © 2003 by Gregory Stock. All rights reserved. Reproduced by permission. www.gregorystock.net.

Many of the public figures trying to shape policy in the life sciences these days—from Francis Fukuyama and Leon Kass to the perennial Jeremy Rifkin—are troubled by recent advances in biotechnology. Nor are they alone in their fears of the new possibilities that are emerging; their angst is even shared by some of the scientists at the vanguard of this research. As we push further into uncharted territory by deciphering and laying bare the workings of life, it is worth asking just what it is that so worries us.

The enormity of coming developments in molecular biology seems obvious, but their magnitude does not require that we respond with fear. We are hardly the first to appreciate the prospects for impending revolutionary developments in science. In 1780, Benjamin Franklin showed a very different attitude, when he wrote to the great English chemist Joseph Priestley, "The rapid progress true science makes occasions my regretting sometimes that I was born so soon. It is impossible to imagine the heights to which may be carried, in a thousand years, the power of man over matter."

Franklin was less bothered by impending changes from the next millennium of scientific discovery than by not being around to witness these amazing possibilities. Today, at the comparatively short remove of 225 years from that letter, the thousand-year span of his forecast seems conservative. But if Franklin could come back and see the extraordinary technologies that have arisen since his death, I suspect it would please him no end.

When we look at the possibilities embodied in the Human Genome Project, which are emblematic of those in proteomics, systems biology, and molecular biology in general, we see that this research is poised to carry humanity to destinations of new imagination. The possibilities a mere century hence are so mind-boggling that many scientists today who do not even believe in God are resorting to religious metaphor to try to communicate what is happening. Three years ago, the announcement of the rough sequence of the human genome provoked widespread commentary about finding the "Holy Grail of Biology," reading the "Book of Life," and breaking the "Code of Codes." This unalloyed enthusiasm, coupled with projections of rapid progress in biomedicine, created soaring biotech valuations until investors began to realize how long and arduous the path might be from identifying gene targets to getting practical results and moving them into the clinic.

The world has not yet shifted beneath our feet. Cancer and heart disease are still the biggest killers. We still get old and suffer the same diseases of aging. The promises of new drugs, gene therapies, and tissue engineering remain unfulfilled.

The excitement about the human genome was reminiscent of 1969, when Neil Armstrong walked on the moon and we were about to race out towards the stars—a vision so perfectly embodied in Stanley Kubrick's classic film "2001: A Space Odyssey." But that date has come and gone, and there is no HAL, and no space odyssey to our own moon, much less the moons of Jupiter. It is hardly surprising that people are wondering whether 35 years from now our children will look back at this moment too and smile about the enthusiasm for regenerative medicine, life extension, and designer babies. Will this all then seem like a crazy dream that brought us precious little?

Genetics and biology are at our core. As we learn to adjust and modify these realms, we are learning to change ourselves.

Technology Reshapes Us

I think not. Genetics and biology are at our core. As we learn to adjust and modify these realms, we are learning to change ourselves. We have already used technology to transform the world around us. The canyons of glass, concrete, and stainless steel in any major city are not the stomping ground of our Pleistocene ancestors. Now our technology is becoming so potent and so precise that we are turning it back on our own selves. And before we're done, we are likely to transform our own biology as much as we have already changed the world around us.

The sense that humanity is at the threshold of reworking its own biology is what troubles so many people. Clearly, medicine and healthcare will be transformed in the process. But these technologies will do much more than that. They will change the way we have children, alter how we manage our emotions, and even modify the human lifespan. Far sooner than people imagine, these core technologies will take us to the very question of what it means to be human.

Research in genomics, proteomics, genetic engineering, and regenerative medicine will be at the heart of these developments, and they will be subject not only to fickle public enthusiasm and angst, but to a tide of regulation, litigation, and political conflict. . . .

Our real fears [arising from advancements in biotechnology] come from more distant possibilities that could be far more difficult and divisive [than near-term social, political, and legal challenges]. Three basic realms are apparent.

Extending the Human Lifespan

The first is the reshaping of our biology. That does not mean that we are somehow going to develop another pair of arms or a set of gills; other aspects of our biology are much more important to us. What if we could unravel the processes of aging and learn to retard or even reverse critical aspects of it? This is a key focus of regenerative medicine, and success would affect virtually every aspect of human society, from family relationships, to educational structures, to the passage of wealth and power from one generation to the next, to the shapes of various social institutions. The potential collapse of social security is the least of it. Nor is this pseudo-science. Steven Austadt, for example, a mainstream biogerontologist at the University of Idaho, believes that the first person who will live to be 150 years old is already alive.

People often tell me they don't think it would be a good idea if we were able to extend the human life span. They are worried that there are too many people on the planet already, that there would be environmental consequences, that life would lose its meaning, that extending one's life would be selfish, or even that all those extra years would be boring. Then they often whisper, "but put me on the list."

Extension of human vitality and life span would be widely embraced if they arrived. William Butler Yeats captured our yearning for immortality eloquently in his poem "Sailing to Byzantium," when he wrote, "Consume my heart away; sick with desire and fastened to a dying animal, it knows not what it is. Gather me into the artifice of eternity."

Extension of human vitality and life span would be widely embraced if they arrived.

This project to dramatically extend the human health span is greatly at odds with the present goals of biogerontology, which are not to buy us more life, but essentially to condense our period of morbidity so that we could live healthy lives and then, within a very narrow period, rapidly deteriorate, like a salmon that has spawned. But the full achievement of this goal would be a nightmare, profoundly at odds with our true aspirations. Imagine how unprepared we would be to leave this world if we lived vitally until 80 and then, within a month or so, died. Not only would this be excruciating, it would leave gaping wounds behind, for sickness and decline prepare us and those around us for our departure. I suspect that given the choice, most people would prefer both a longer and a healthier life than either one by itself.

Reliance on Pharmacology

A second area that troubles many people is our increasing reliance on pharmacology not just to heal ourselves, but to manage our emotional states as well. Such "cosmetic psychopharmacology" falls outside of regenerative medicine, but will be increasingly challenging in coming decades. Ritalin, Viagra, Prozac, and other such drugs are only clumsy baby steps. The potential is now emerging to short-circuit the emotional programs that have arisen in our evolutionary history to direct human behavior in ways that further survival and reproduction. It is no accident that we like sugar, that sex feels good, that we are strongly attached to our family, that success can bring a sense of fulfillment.

What would happen if we could take a cocktail of drugs that made us feel contented and fulfilled in whatever we were doing, and had no noticeable physiological side effects? Would we be able to resist using it, and if we didn't, who would we be? Why would we do what we do? What would motivate and drive our behavior? Whatever agents we are able or unable to fashion in this arena, it is clear that the lines between medical pharmaceuticals and illicit "recreational" drugs will become ever more obscure in the years ahead.

Choosing Our Children's Genes

A third area in which biotechnology is challenging us is reproduction. Our focus on this is not surprising, given that the passage of life from one generation to the next is so central to people's perceptions of who they are.

As we understand the constellations of genes that influence our identities, potentials, vulnerabilities, and temperaments, we will want to make choices about the genetic constitutions of our children. Setting aside familiar low-tech methods of mate selection such as arranged marriages and romantic love, and various coming refinements like computer dating, we can anticipate the arrival of three high-tech procedures to consciously choose our children's genes.

The first is reproductive cloning. Media obsession with this is due more to the symbolism of such an alteration of human reproduction than to any plausible consequences of its occurrence. After all, here is a technology that does not yet exist for humans—indeed, no one has yet used nuclear transfer to create viable embryos even in nonhuman primates—and yet enormous global attention has greeted the flimsiest of claims about the procedure. Even more importantly, fear that someone, somewhere, might clone a child has generated serious attempts to criminalize basic biomedical research in regenerative medicine, endangering the hopes of real people with real diseases and real suffering.

Part of this fear no doubt comes from an exaggeration of the consequences of reproductive cloning. Reproductive cloning will likely occur within 5 to 10 years, long before mainstream medical professionals view the procedure as safe, and it will be reported on numerous occasions before it is achieved, as in the case of the Raelian scam in December of 2002. But when reproductive cloning does occur, it is hardly going to be a cataclysmic event. Given the challenges of the procedure, it will necessarily occur on a very small scale, and there will be a long lag before it is seen as safe enough by any but a few driven souls. A few babies may be harmed, of course, but it is hard to see how the creation of a delayed identical twin is going to bring down our civilization, and it is hard to see how fears of cloning could possibly justify stopping embryonic stem-cell research, which seems to hold such promise. Our real concern should not be that some fringe group will attempt to clone a child somewhere, but that fears about this will be purposely fanned by those who wish to control the future of reproductive medicine and biotechnology in general.

Another means of selecting our children's genetic constitutions is embryo screening or "preimplantation genetic diagnosis (PGD)." In this already common procedure, a single cell is removed from a six- or eight-celled embryo *in vitro* and a genetic test is performed on it. The results are then used to decide whether to implant that embryo or discard it in favor of another. PGD has been in use for 10 years to avoid serious diseases such as cystic fibrosis. Such screening procedures are far more important than cloning, and will come into widespread use once *in vitro* fertilization [IVF] progresses to the point at which it is feasible to freeze immature oocytes. Then, a woman could have a simple ovarian biopsy to collect thousands of eggs, freeze them, and bank them, so that years later, she could thaw and mature them *in vitro* and fertilize them with her partner's sperm. If she believes in letting nature take its course, she might choose one of the resultant embryos at random for implantation, but I suspect it will be far more common to first screen the banked embryos for genetic diseases or even temperament and personality traits.

Such technology will greatly impact human reproduction as it spreads from the infertile who are already using IVF, to the affluent who are worried about genetic disease, to the population at large. PGD will also affect reproduction as the technology moves from simple screening for disease toward screenings for lesser vulnerabilities like severe depression and finally for traits of personality and temperament. Moreover, the technology will probably become so potent that the biggest pressure may be to make it available to everyone, rather than to ban it.

The ultimate means of changing human reproduction is, clearly, through direct germline intervention—direct alteration of the genetics of the first cell of the human embryo. This would be the beginning of conscious human design. . . .

Humans Want to Use Technology to Enhance Our Lives

In the manipulation of human embryos for purposes of screening and enhancement, not everything that can be done should or will be done. But international polls show that 25 to

80% of parents in every country examined say that they would enhance the physical or mental capacities of their children through these technologies if they could do so safely. Given that a significant number of people everywhere regard such technology as beneficial, that it will be feasible in thousands of laboratories throughout the world, and that its use will be so difficult to monitor, the question is not whether such technology will arrive, but when and where it will, and what it will look like.

Humanity will go down this path for two reasons. The first is that there is no need to pursue the technology directly. It will emerge from the basic biomedical research now underway at our most prestigious institutions.

The second reason we will proceed is that we are human, and have always used technology to try to enhance our lives. We plant; we build; we mine; we hunt; we dam, and for as long as we have been able, we've altered ourselves as well. We cut our hair, straighten our teeth, pierce our bodies, tattoo our skin, fix our noses. We use drugs to ease pain, lose weight, stay awake, go to sleep, or just get high. The idea that we will long forego better and more potent ways of modifying ourselves is every bit as much a denial of what the past tells us about who we are, as to imagine that we would use these technologies without fretting about them.

[W]e are human, and have always used technology to try to enhance our lives. We plant; we build; we mine; we dam, and for as long as we have been able, we've altered ourselves as well.

Efforts to Ban Will Fail

Worrying about these new technologies has considerable survival value, but efforts to ban them will not succeed. If we draw regulatory guidelines that are too restrictive, it will merely shift research elsewhere, drive it from view, and reserve the technologies themselves for the wealthy, who are in the best position to circumvent restrictions. Such policies thus would mean both relinquishing control over these new technologies by handing them off to others, and delaying whatever benefits emerge from them. As with so many other extensions of human power, no matter how much debate occurs, there will be no consensus about changing human reproduction, expanding human potential, extending human longevity, using drugs to alter human emotion, or simply screening human embryos. Each will remain contentious because it touches us and our vision of the human future so deeply. Our responses are driven by our history, religion, culture, philosophy, and politics.

A bioethics advisory commission may pretend that moratoria and additional debate will allow us to reach consensus, but this is delusion. The two poles of the debate are too far apart. To some, changing human reproduction is an invasion by the inhuman. It violates their views of what is most sacred. To others, such advances represent the flowering of our humanity, a chance to transcend aspects of our biology in ways other generations could only dream of.

Weighing the possibilities of regenerative medicine are easy for those in these extreme camps. Christian fundamentalists will oppose them with all their fiber, and Transhumanists will embrace them wholeheartedly, pushing to have regenerative technologies introduced as rapidly as possible. The people most conflicted by the prospects of changing human reproduction are those who are involved in the work of bringing it about and are concerned about some of its applications.

Ian Wilmut, for example, who cloned the sheep Dolly—the first mammal to be cloned—and has probably done more than anyone to bring about mammalian cloning, is deeply troubled by the possibility of its application to humans. It is hard to imagine, though, that a human will not one day be cloned. These technologies will arrive. They will help many people, and they no doubt will cause injuries as well. Such is generally the case with new technologies. Our challenge will not be how we deal with cloning, genetic screening, or any specific technology, but whether we have the courage to continue to face the possibilities of the future and accept the risks inherent in such exploration, or whether we pull back in fear and relinquish this effort to other, braver souls in other regions of the world.

The real worry is that these technologies will succeed so gloriously that they will create a host of seductive possibilities we can not resist.

One of the most dangerous paths would be that represented by the precautionary principle, which posits that we should be certain that technology is absolutely safe before we attempt to use it. This recipe for stasis is not an option, but were it possible, it would deny us the benefits of new developments simply because their development entailed risk. None of the progress of recent centuries could have taken place under a regime embracing such a principle.

The political choices we make today will be very important, not because they will determine whether these new technologies arrive, which is not in question, but because they will determine our ability to influence the development of these technologies. Germany has banned work on embryos, and now exerts no influence in that realm.

Why We Worry

Let us return to the question we began with: What are we really afraid of? Critics are not particularly concerned that these technologies—including those of regenerative medicine—will fail or that someone somewhere will be injured by them. That would be a relief in many ways, because then the technologies would fade away or at least be greatly slowed.

The real worry is that these technologies will succeed so gloriously that they will create a host of seductive possibilities we can not resist. What strikes fear into the hearts of critics is that we as individuals and as a society will see so much benefit in these technologies that we will embrace them. Then, critics will have to face their real fears:

Their first fear is of ourselves. They worry that we will abuse these technologies. But here, I take comfort from the protections that come from liberal governments and open markets. Together, they act against both the grand social engineering projects that totalitarian regimes sometimes inflict on their citizenry, and against the many bizarre dangers that often populate bioethical debate. The former violate our guarantees of personal freedoms, and the latter have too few potential adherents to inspire commercial development that would figure significantly in our future.

Society has navigated technological change before, and will muddle through once again. The new biomedical technologies described here are not like nuclear weapons, with which one mistake can vaporize millions of innocents. In truth, we need to make mistakes and learn from them to gain the wisdom to handle these new possibilities wisely. Most people will show common sense when it comes to making choices about these things in their own lives—far more, perhaps, than the government committees whose members do not suffer the consequences of the mistakes they make. But progress in these realms will not be smooth, and people will get hurt. That is the way both biological and technological evolution work.

Another fear is of the philosophical implications of these coming possibilities. People worry that they may change our sense of who we are. This is probably the least valid basis for making public policy about new biotechnology, because our sense of what it means to be human will so obviously be changed by a broad range of technological advance in the years ahead. If we could stop biotechnology dead in its tracks, other technologies would still reshape our society. When we contemplate the future, we should remember that our great grandparents would not be comfortable in the world of today, and yet most of us would not want to live in their time. So it will be with our future. We may not like it, but our descendants will, and they will probably look back at the present era as primitive and uninviting.

A third fear is that we will be forced to make difficult choices as these new genetic and reproductive technologies arise. But such choices are part of growing up. Humanity is leaving its childhood and moving into its adolescence as our powers infuse into realms that were hitherto beyond our reach.

As we learn to use regenerative medicine to extend our vitality and stave off death, we will need to decide more often when to forgo such technology and let death come, and yet, we are not good at making such decisions even with today's limited technology. When people talk about extending the human life span, they frequently begin to worry about immortality. But a chasm lies between doubling our life spans and achieving immortality.

The beginning of life will present us with tough decisions also. Being able to screen embryos means we will have to make judgments about our potential future children and pick one over another, something we are very uncomfortable with.

The biggest fear, though, is that we will have to relinquish control, or rather, acknowledge that we do not really have control over humanity's future. The long-term consequences of the self-directed evolution now underway are not something we can plan, because our course hinges too much on the character of future technologies we cannot yet glimpse and on the values of future humans we cannot yet understand.

Moving Forward with Courage

It is ironic that accepting the technological path I have described is a deeply spiritual choice. Embarking on this voyage to we-know-not-where is a far greater act of faith than trying to barricade against it by insisting that we should not play God. It is clear that we already do play God in many ways, from using antibiotics to flying airplanes.

I have mentioned the largest fears of those who would hold back coming advances in regenerative medicine and other realms of biotechnology. In my view, the dangers from these possibilities pale beside the risk that we will succumb to our fears and shrink from these new technologies delaying beneficial might-have-beens. Think of the millions of unperceived injuries that would have resulted from policies that delayed for a decade the arrival of the polio vaccine.

[T]he dangers from these possibilities pale beside the risk that we will succumb to our fears and shrink from these new technologies.

We have entered a new millennium, and long before the next, future humans will look back at our era. They may see it as a challenging, difficult, turbulent time, which of course it is, but I think they will primarily see it as the unique, extraordinary, glorious instant when the very foundations of their lives—better and longer lives with better health and greater choices—were laid down. It is a remarkable privilege to be here to observe this critical transition in the history of life. But, of course, we are more than observers; we are the architects of a broad set of changes that will soon reshape human life and our understanding of it. In my view, we should be proud of this. But don't think for a moment that these shifts will not challenge us, because we are also the objects of these changes.

In 430 BC, the Athenian historian Thucydides seemed to have foreseen our challenge and our calling when he wrote, "The bravest are surely those who have the clearest vision of what is before them, glory and danger alike, and yet notwithstanding go out and meet it."

11

Biotechnology Must Not Be Used to Alter Human Nature

Marc D. Guerra

Marc D. Guerra is a teacher of theology at Assumption College in Worcester, Massachusetts.

Marc D. Guerra discusses Life, Liberty, and the Defense of Human Dignity: The Challenge of Bioethics, *a book by Leon R. Kass. According to Kass, the growing ability of biotechnology to change our nature threatens our humanity. Although biotechnology has provided a way for us to live healthier and longer lives, some advances in biotechnology threaten to alter the "very face of our humanity." Biotechnology associated with "designer babies" would be the type that Kass concludes would flatten our souls.*

Leon Kass has described himself as a strange man who writes strange and untimely books. Given the intellectual condition of the contemporary academy, this is by no means a bad thing. Trained professionally as a physician and biochemist, Kass has, without formal academic training, taught courses in philosophy and literature for the past twenty-eight years at the University of Chicago. A prolific essayist, he has published books on the proper relation of biology and human affairs, the connection between eating and the perfection of human nature, and the deepest meanings of courtship and marriage.

But the real reason why Kass seems so strange today is that he defends the dignity of our given human nature in a world that is transformed almost daily by advances in science and technology.

Life, Liberty, and the Defense of Dignity is largely a collection of reworked, previously published essays on biotechnology—one of which originally appeared in *First Things* ("L'Chaim and Its Limits: Why Not Immortality?" May 2001). In this book, the Chairman of the President's Council on Bioethics offers a penetrating and unnerving reflection on how biotechnology's growing ability to alter our nature fundamentally threatens our dignity as human beings. Biotechnology is, as Kass shows, something of a mixed blessing. It has allowed many of us to live longer and healthier lives, something Kass believes we should be most grateful for. At the same time, some emerging biotechnologies—especially in neuroscience and psychopharmacology—threaten to technologically alter the very face of our humanity. As Kass jarringly puts it in his Introduction, the burgeoning biotech revolution has already brought us to a point where "human nature itself lies on the operating table, ready for alteration, for eugenic and neuropsychic 'enhancement,' for wholesale redesign."

Flattening Our Souls

In Kass' view, this kind of technological enhancement and redesign ultimately will result in the flattening of our souls. By pursuing physical health as the greatest of human goods, we will inevitably end up sacrificing the moral and spiritual goods that give meaning and dignity to our lives. The degraded and dehumanized "Brave New World" of soma and Bokanovskification that Aldous Huxley so vividly described two generations ago seems closer with each passing day.

Western societies have largely been unwilling to face the all-too-human consequences of this looming posthuman future. Seduced by promises of even bigger and better biotechnologies in the years to come, we have opted not to think about what is really at stake in the biotech revolution. However, given the recent extraordinary proliferation of biotechnologies, from the completion of the Human Genome Project to our growing expertise in the science of cloning, the time has come for everyone who cares about the preservation of our humanity to recognize what is at stake. In this effort, Kass' elegantly written and thought-provoking book will undoubtedly be of much help.

Consequently, modern science would effectively transform our view of nature itself.

The Problem of Technology

Kass begins his book with a reflection on "the problem of technology and liberal democracy." The two have something of a symbiotic relationship. On the one hand, genuine technological progress presupposes the kind of intellectual and economic freedom that liberal democracy secures. On the other, liberal societies must rely upon technology for assistance in everything from supplying healthy and affordable foods, to sustaining great numbers of people, to developing new and improved military technologies. But technology also creates its own set of problems. Take the case of medical science's increased ability to push back the frontiers of death. As medical science has helped us live healthier and longer lives, our society has had to struggle to figure out how to take care of a citizenry whose longevity continually increases. Like so many other things in life, technological "progress" is not immune to the law of unintended consequences.

That we view technology as a "problem" at all shows the remarkable extent to which we have internalized modern science's mechanized and reductionist account of the world. As Kass shows, the greatest problem posed by today's "brave new biology" does not come from the technologies it produces, but rather from the scientific view from which it is derived. To understand just how deep the problem of biotechnology runs, Kass points out, it must be viewed in the larger context of the revolutionary character of modern science.

Building on the analysis of thinkers such as Leo Strauss and Hans Jonas, Kass offers a rich reflection on the "philosophical foundations" of modern science. The philosophical architects of modern natural science, such as Bacon and Descartes, believed that if science were to successfully minister to human beings' needs, it would have to alter its basic theoretical posture. Whereas ancient science tried to discover *what* things are, modern science would now focus on *how* they worked. Knowledge would be seen as desirable not for its own sake, but because it showed how things could be manipulated to fulfill our many desires. Consequently, modern science would effectively transform our view of nature itself. Nature could no longer be seen as "animated, purposive, and striving," but as mere "dead matter in motion," matter that could, and should, be mastered in order to bring about, in Bacon's famous phrase, "the relief of man's estate." The very idea of modern science, as Kass shows, "contains manipulability at its theoretical core."

Biotechnology is a variation on this larger scientific theme. But it is a particularly dangerous variation, since it allows for the technological manipulation of the manipulator himself. Biotechnology thus paves the way for the complete "medicalization of life and death." Armed with increased knowledge of how our genes and brains work, we are now in a position to be the subjects of our own manipulations. This is the deceptive promise lurking behind the biotech project. Through neuropharmaceuticals and germ-line therapy, we are told, we will be able to smooth out all of human nature's rough edges, thus making us completely at home in the world and with ourselves.

The Problem of Biotechnology

If Kass' diagnosis of the problem of technology is correct, and it rings completely true to this reviewer, there is something deeply unsettling about our current situation. The problem of biotechnology is something that we are remarkably ill equipped to deal with today, if for no other reason than that we are generally unaware of the way that modern science has shaped the very way we see ourselves and the world. What Kass indirectly shows is that even such admirable defenders of human dignity as Francis Fukuyama and James Q. Wilson, who argue that the solution to the problem of biotechnology ultimately lies in enacting sound regulations, radically underestimate the true magnitude of the biotech challenge. And the same could be said about those thinkers who primarily approach the question of biotechnology from the perspective of Pope John Paul II's rich analysis of "the culture of death." As insightful and instructive as this analysis is, it too tends to see biotechnology as the source of some particularly dehumanizing practices and not as the product of an all-encompassing scientific view of the world. For liberal societies, unfortunately, there is no quick and easy solution to the "problem" of biotechnology, precisely because it is rooted in the very premises of the modern scientific project itself.

Kass believes that if we are going to confront the challenge of biotechnology seriously and effectively we will have to develop a "more natural biology and anthropology" than the one we have now. Only such a "biologically informed anthropology" can remind us of just what we have to lose through the biotechnological transformation of our humanity. Kass goes a long way in this book towards laying the groundwork for such a biology—and he here builds on some of the arguments he first made in *Towards a More Natural Science* (1985). But Kass also knows that even a biology that recognizes that human life is lived "not just physically, but psychically, socially, and spiritually" cannot address all of the challenges posed by the brave new future envisioned by biotechnology. As he shows in the book's final chapter, "The Permanent Limitations of Biology," no "purely biological" account of man will ever be able to do justice to our lived experience as human beings. There will always be "permanent limits" to what biology can tell us about our lives. The task of defending morality and human dignity and of adjudicating between the claims of the body and soul consequently will "always remain the work of a largely autonomous ethical and political science." A more natural biology may be able to tell us much about "the loves of life," but it finally cannot tell us how we should live with life's different loves.

For cloning is, in principle, corrosive of the natural ties that connect generations and the erotic desire to take part in an act that transcends our own finite existence.

But because he is aware of the limits of just how far biology can take us, Kass sheds a good deal of light on what is really good and dignified about human life. Indeed, as he points out in a series of chapters on such biotech practices as in vitro fertilization, organ transplantation, cloning, and euthanasia, the cultivation of human dignity actually requires us to live "with and against necessity, struggling to meet it, not to overcome it." And yet Kass is clearly no Stoic. He sees too much good in human life to accept Stoicism's claim that we should always remain somewhat detached from the world. Like Pascal and Flannery O'Connor, he thinks that a truly human life requires us to live well with necessity and enjoy those goods such as love and friendship that transcend necessity—though, in contrast to Pascal and O'Connor, there remains a tension in his thought about how these two things finally fit together.

Human Costs of Cloning

Kass is at his best when reflecting on the two poles of human biological life, birth and death. His treatment of the "human costs" of cloning is second to none. Cutting through the too "familiar political thickets . . . of pro-life and pro-choice," he shows that the new science of cloning is emphatically not a matter of reproductive rights and technologies. Cloning would allow us to become our own creators, designing our descendants through the technological tyranny of eugenics, thus making possible a kind of evil that is even more perverse than the willful destruction of nascent human life. This is, for Kass, the "political" reason why we should ban human cloning—and he makes a strong case that our initial natural "repugnance" to cloning offers an entranceway to opening up larger questions about the overall desirability of the biotech project.

But he also suggests that what is most pernicious about cloning is that it threatens to extinguish those profound erotic longings that find their fullest expression in human coupling. For cloning is, in principle, corrosive of the natural ties that connect generations and the erotic desire to take part in an act that transcends our own finite existence. The society that condones cloning and denies "the profundity of sex," Kass argues, has already taken a giant step towards removing eros from human life altogether.

Biotech's pursuit of what Kass calls "the immortality project" similarly threatens our ability to live a dignified human life. Advances in the use of human growth hormone, stem cells, and the genetic switches that control the aging process hold out the possibility that some day we will be able to radically retard the aging process. But what will be lost if death becomes an increasingly rare and remote occurrence? What will happen to life when we will no longer have to wonder, in the words of the Psalmist, about "the number of our days"? Reflecting on the mysterious connection between mortality and morality, Kass argues that awareness of our mortality adds depth and weight to our lives and points to the grounds of the kind of knowing self-sacrifice that cultivates "the peculiarly human beauty of . . . virtue and moral excellence."

What temporal immortality really would allow for is the endless enjoyment of the present, a freezing of time in which we would always have the chance to enjoy the goods life has to offer. However, even if such a life becomes possible, it will not bring us real happiness. "Man longs not so much for deathlessness as for wholeness, wisdom, goodness, and godliness." This is, as Kass observes, the shared message of the wisdom expressed in Aristophanes' tale of the circle men, Socratic philosophy, and the Bible. As Kass argues, each of these longings—not just the desire for wisdom, as some of Kass' early writings suggested—points to the fact that our desire for human wholeness cannot be satisfied by any quantity of earthly life.

The last observation points to the real reason why even the kind of biology that Kass develops is finally incapable of supplying the grounds for a wholly satisfying natural ethic. For the truth of the matter is that the type of "wholeness" that biblical religion speaks of is fundamentally different from the wholeness that comes from finding our Aristophanic other half or from the Socratic contemplation of wisdom. It is a wholeness that embraces the good of the entire person, body and soul, and that perfects—not smoothes out—the imperfections of our nature. But if this is the kind of wholeness that we really seek, we will never be truly at home in this world, no matter how well we live with necessity. As Peter Lawler has recently argued, perhaps finally only theological anthropology is capable of giving a humanly satisfying account of how we can really live well in a world where the reach of our natural desires will always exceed our grasp.

12

Concerns About Biotechnology Altering Human Nature Are Groundless

Kenan Malik

Kenan Malik is an author, broadcaster, essayist, and lecturer. He appears regularly on BBC Radio 4 in Britain. His latest book, From Fatwa to Jihad: The Rushdie Affair and Its Legacy, *was shortlisted for the 2010 George Orwell Book Prize.*

Francis Fukuyama's argument that human principles, namely capitalist values, are at risk of being rendered unrecognizable by the advancement of biotechnology holds little weight when the history of humanity is examined. The doubling of lifespan over the past two centuries, for example, has not resulted in the collapse of society. As humans are empowered to interact with genetics in an intentional and purposeful way, it follows then that biotech developments will not ruin the basic moral foundations of society. Protecting innate human nature at the cost of important medical advancement is a mistake.

Capitalism, Francis Fukuyama announced more than a decade ago, is the promised land at the End of History. The collapse of the Soviet Union confirmed that there was neither an alternative to the market, nor a possibility of transcending capitalism.

Not even the events of September 11 [2001], which have led many critics to mock the 'End of History' thesis, have given Fukuyama cause to change his mind. The end of history, Fukuyama argues, means not the termination of conflict, simply the recognition that nothing can improve upon capitalism. Why? Because, as he puts it in *Our Posthuman Future*, capitalist institutions 'are grounded in assumptions about human nature that are far more realistic than those of their competitors'.

Yet even Fukuyama has come to worry that the reports of History's death might have been a mite exaggerated. Capitalism, he fears, is undermining its own foundations. Not, as Marx thought, through the agency of the working class, but as a result of the unrestricted advance of science and technology. Science, and in particular biotechnology, has, Fukuyama believes, the potential to change the kinds of beings we are, and in so doing to 'recommence history', propelling us from a human to a posthuman world. From the end of history to the end of human nature as we know it.

[B]iotechnology has, [Francis] Fukuyama believes, the potential to change the kinds of beings we are.

A Misguided Argument

Fukuyama's argument runs something like this. Human values are rooted in human nature. Human nature is rooted in our biological being, in particular in our genes. Messing around with human biology could alter human nature, transform our values and undermine capitalism. 'What is ultimately at stake with biotechnology', Fukuyama declares, 'is . . . the very grounding of the human moral sense.' We therefore need international regulation to obstruct any technological advance that might 'disrupt either the unity or the continuity of human nature, and thereby the human rights that are based upon it.'

While most worried about genetic engineering, other technologies also concern Fukuyama. Cloning is an 'unnatural form' of reproduction that might create 'unnatural urges' in a parent whose spouse has been cloned. Prozac is giving women 'more of the alpha-male feeling that comes with high serotonin levels', while Ritalin is making 'young boys . . . sit still' even though 'nature never designed them to behave that way.'

Even attempt[ing] slow down the ageing process is 'unnatural' and fraught with danger. The world, Fukuyama believes, may soon be divided 'between a North whose political tone is set by elderly women' (since women tend to live longer than men) and 'a South driven by . . . super-empowered angry young men.' The consequence will not simply be more days like September 11, but also a disinclination on the part of the West to use force in response, since women are apparently naturally less aggressive than men.

Such fears may seem to carry all the scholarly weight of a Hollywood dystopian fantasy (*Gattaca* meets *The Invasion of the Body Snatchers*, perhaps). If capitalism is as natural as Fukuyama claims, how is it that for virtually the whole of human history people abided by entirely different sets of values and beliefs? And what exactly worries Fukuyama about genetic engineering? That we will be turned into a race of beings who believe that the market may not be the best way to promote human flourishing? Or (God forbid) that we will lose our attachment to the sanctity of property?

As for the dangers of longevity, life expectancy has doubled in the past two centuries—without any evidence of social breakdown. Nor is there any evidence that the extension of the franchise to women at the beginning of the twentieth century made that century any less violent than the nineteenth.

Absurd though such arguments may seem to be, at the heart of Fukuyama's book is a discussion, not of biotechnology, but of what it is to be human. To understand his alarmism about biotechnology, we have to understand his confusions over human nature.

A Flawed View of Humanity

For Fukuyama, humans as a species possess an inner essence or nature, which he defines as 'the sum total of the behaviour and characteristics that are typical of the human species, arising from genetic rather than environmental factors.' From this perspective, humans seem little more than sophisticated animals. 'Many of the attributes that were once held to be unique to human beings—including language, culture, reason, consciousness, and the like—are', Fukuyama believes, 'characteristic of a wide variety of nonhuman animals'.

Human values are . . . not fixed in our nature, but emerge from our capacity to transcend that nature.

At the same time, though, Fukuyama presents humans as exceptional beings. While all animals have a nature, only humans possess 'dignity'. Dignity gives humans a 'superior . . . moral status that raises us all above the rest of animal creation and yet makes us equals of one another qua [in the capacity of] human beings.' Such dignity, Fukuyama believes, resides in a mysterious 'Factor X' which is the 'essential human quality' that remains after 'all of a person's contingent and accidental characteristics' have been stripped away. It is Factor X that Fukuyama wants to preserve from the clutches of biotechnologists.

And therein lies the problem. 'Factor X' appears to be both the same as human nature—the 'essence' of our humanity—and also that which makes humans entirely distinct from the rest of nature. Indeed, Fukuyama suggests that somewhere along the human evolutionary journey there occurred 'a very important qualitative, if not ontological, leap', that came to separate Man and Beast.

Fukuyama is right, I think, to assert the 'dual character' of human existence, of humans as both animal and yet more-than-animal. But he seems not to recognise what this means for the concept of human nature. If humans are qualitatively distinct from the rest of the natural world, then the human 'essence' cannot be simply rooted in nature.

What sets humans apart is not some mysterious Factor X hidden somewhere in our biology but rather our ability to act as conscious agents. Uniquely among organisms, humans are both objects of nature and subjects that can, to some extent at least, shape our own fate. We are biological beings, and under the purview of biological and physical laws. But we are also conscious beings with purpose and agency, traits the possession of which allow us to design ways of breaking the constraints of biological and physical laws.

It is only because humans are conscious agents that we possess moral values. As Fukuyama himself observes, 'Only human beings can formulate, debate, and modify abstract rules of justice'. This is why we should not 'confuse human politics with the social behaviour of any other species'.

The real debate is not about whether biotechnology will undermine our values, but about the kind of values to which we aspire.

Human values in other words, are not fixed in our nature, but emerge from our capacity to transcend that nature. To a certain degree, Fukuyama recognises this. Violence, he suggests, 'may be natural to human beings'. But so, too, is 'the propensity to control and channel violence'. Humans are capable of 'reasoning about their situation' and of 'understanding the need to create rules and institutions that constrain violence'. Humans, therefore, possess the capacity to rise above their natural inclinations and, through the use of reason, to shape their values.

But if this is so, then no amount of biotechnological intervention will transform our fundamental values. What may

transform them, however, is the kind of pessimism that Fukuyama expresses in his End of Human Nature thesis.

Taking Responsibility for Our Values

Fukuyama rightly worries about the 'medicalisation of
society'—the inclination to view personal, social and political
problems in biological or medical terms. In part, at least, this
arises from the growing tendency of our age to view humans
as weak-willed, sick or damaged, as victims lacking the capacity to transcend their situation, either individually or collec-
tively. Biotechnology, Fukuyama believes, can only entrench
such perceptions, making it easier for individuals who 'would
like to absolve themselves of responsibility for their actions.'

But Fukuyama's own belief that values are embedded in
our biology, and should be ring-fenced for protection, can
only exacerbate this problem. If our values were simply evolved
adaptations, then the notion of moral responsibility would indeed appear to be fragile. And what would then be wrong
with popping a pill or performing a bit of genetic surgery to
improve our moral condition?

The real debate is not about whether biotechnology will
undermine our values, but about the kind of values to which
we aspire. Do we want a human-centred morality rooted in
concrete human needs (such as for solutions to brain disorders and genetic illnesses like Alzheimer's, Parkinson's and
cystic fibrosis)? Or are we happy with a moral code that un-
dermines the promise of medical advance in the name of a
mythical human nature?

For Fukuyama, 'There are good prudential reasons to defer
to the natural order of things and not to think that human
beings can easily improve upon it through casual intervention'.
But why should the 'natural order of things' be better than
human creation? After all, we only need medicine because nature has left us with jerry-built bodies that tend constantly to

break down with headaches and backaches, cancers and coronaries, schizophrenia and depression.

'If the artificial is not better than that natural', John Stuart Mill once asked, 'to what end are all the arts of life?' 'It's unnatural' has always been the cry of those who seek to obstruct progress and restrain 'the arts of life'. It's an argument no more valid in response to biotechnology than it was in response to vaccination, heart transplants or IVF [in vitro fertilization] treatment. The 'duty of man', as Mill put it, 'is the same in respect to his own nature as in respect to the nature of other things, namely not to follow but to amend it.'

13

The Designer Baby Business Violates Christian Principles

Michael Poore

Michael Poore is a writer and lecturer, focusing on the relationship between bioethics and biotechnology and contemporary culture. He is founder and executive director of The Humanitas Project: A Center for Bioethic Education. His blog is "The Humanitas Forum on Christianity and Culture" (www.humanitas .org).

The designer baby business does not seek to provide medical aid to the unhealthy, but rather capitalizes on the desire of parents to hand-pick desirable characteristics for their children. The unregulated system currently in place encourages clinics to cater to the crudest wishes of parents, including cases where parents seek to have a baby who shares their disability. An example of this behavior is the non-hearing lesbian couple who enlisted the services of the designer baby business. They subjected their child not only to an unnatural family home, but also to a life of deafness. The argument that individuals should be free to alter the natural order of life is a selfish one. The Christian understanding of unconditional love and acceptance is the only answer to an otherwise narcissistic business.

D esigner babies! As the name implies, these babies are made to a certain specification—to have certain traits, but not others.

Michael Poore, "Baby Shopping: The Clash of Worldviews in Bioethics," The *Humanitas* Project, 2007. http://www.humanitas.org. Copyright © 2007 by The *Humanitas* Project. All rights reserved. Reproduced by permission. First published at BreakPoint.org. Used with permission.

Some of these babies are produced for parents in search of a healthy baby—a baby without a genetic disease.

Other parents want a baby that *has* a disability—a baby with deafness or dwarfism, just like themselves.

Still others want a baby of a particular sex—a girl, please . . . no, we prefer a boy.

Yet other parents want to increase their chances of having a child with high intelligence, athletic ability, or physical beauty.

The Crude Business of Choice

Making designer babies is a crude business that seeks to allow only children with certain characteristics to be born. In some cases, sperm or egg donors are used to improve the chances of having a child with desired traits. In other cases, genetic screening is used to cull out embryos or babies with undesirable traits.

Like all businesses, the designer baby business is built on satisfying a variety of customer desires. It gives parents the ability—although a crude and limited ability—to choose their children in much the same way they shop for a computer.

Making designer babies is a crude business that seeks to allow only children with certain characteristics to be born.

Although it is part of the medical establishment, the goal of the designer baby project is not to make the sick or disabled well. Even when it aims at the birth of a healthy baby, it does not produce healthy babies by healing. Healthy babies are born simply because the unhealthy are eliminated: "Unhealthy" embryos are discarded in the lab, and "imperfect" babies are aborted in the womb.

Like the rest of the $3 billion-per-year fertility industry, the designer baby business is largely unregulated. It appears to be limited only by the current state of the technology, the desires of parents, their ability to pay, and the availability of a clinic willing to comply with their wishes.

And most clinics are willing to comply with about any request a customer makes. A recent survey of the fertility industry by Johns Hopkins University showed that, of the clinics offering embryo screening in conjunction with *in vitro* fertilization, 80 percent would do non-medical sex selection of embryos if requested by parents.

This means that they would select and implant embryos for no other reason than that the parents preferred one sex to the other, thus consigning embryos of the unwanted sex to destruction, either by disposal or in research. Remarkably, in 2005 these same clinics provided non-medical sex selection in 9 percent of the cases that used genetic screening in combination with *in vitro* fertilization.

Interestingly, this data on sex selection did not spark debate either in the mainstream media or among bloggers. Perhaps shopping for a baby of a specific sex has become an accepted practice following a short flurry of media commentary, including a *Newsweek* cover story, in early 2004.

The Hopkins study did, however, stimulate debate about the ethics of making crippled children. It found that 3 percent of the clinics surveyed had used genetic screening to enable parents to select an embryo "*for* the presence of a particular disease or disability . . . in order that the child would share that characteristic with the parents."

Deafness as Parental Choice

While the Hopkins survey may have triggered the recent skirmish in the biotech culture wars, the debate about disabled designer babies is not new. In early 2002 a Maryland couple announced the birth of their second child, a boy named Gauvin, whom they hoped would be deaf.

The couple's justification for wanting a deaf baby? Their desire to "have a baby like us." They are both deaf, and so is their 5-year-old daughter.

Having two deaf children was no coincidence for this deaf lesbian couple, Sharon Duchesneau and Candace McCullough. They had decided to use artificial insemination by a deaf donor, and they turned to a friend who is profoundly deaf and from a family with five generations of deafness.

For Duchesneau and McCullough, having a baby like themselves is more than simply having a baby who cannot hear. They do not consider deafness a disability. It is a normal part of their culture and not a medical condition to be fixed.

As members of Deaf culture, with a capital D, they see deafness as a cultural identity. It is a minority culture that establishes its identity around the use of American Sign Language, its own language. So, for Duchesneau and McCullough, having deaf children is about having children that belong to their own minority culture. In more personal terms, it is about having a baby that can "enjoy what we enjoy."

A baby that can "enjoy what we enjoy." "A deaf baby would be a special blessing." Having a deaf child "would be a wonderful experience." Such comments are a prominent theme of the extensive 2002 *Washington Post Magazine* account of Gauvin McCullough's birth.

[T]here is something perverse in wanting a child that is limited to the enjoyment of what the parents can enjoy.

Of course, all parents hope to share a significant portion of their lives—their beliefs, pleasures, and interests—with their children. But there is something perverse in wanting a child that is limited to the enjoyment of what the parents can enjoy. Their logic: If we can't hear Mozart, we can be better parents to a child that cannot hear Mozart, either.

But if their child were blind, Duchesneau and McCullough would probably try to have that fixed. "I want to be the same as my child," said Candace McCullough. Consequently, Gauvin was denied a hearing aid that, if used at a very young age, could possibly help develop some hearing in one ear.

For Duchesneau and McCullough, there is the added sad perversity of being a lesbian couple. By nature, the two of them cannot reproduce. So, a sperm donor had to be found to father the children they wanted, children who will grow up knowing who their father is but without his being present to *be* their father. Not only have they crippled their children physically, they have also crippled them socially, emotionally, and spiritually.

Only the Christian message of love—of one's neighbor, of the weak, of God and His created order—is powerful enough to counter the distorted desires of the designer baby project.

Christian Love Provides the Solution

All of this is rather self-centered, even narcissistic. And from this self-centeredness flows a host of major moral and ethical issues—issues common to the entire designer baby project. What are the responsibilities and obligations of parenting? Where do these duties come from? Do parents have a right to a baby, even a certain *kind* of baby? Are children to be viewed as gifts, or as projects? How does making designer babies alter the parent-child relationship? In sum, what is the meaning of *love?* Is proper parental love conditional to some quality standard achieved in the child?

How these issues are resolved is, for countless embryos in the lab and babies in the womb, a matter of life or death.

In the designer baby project, ethical decisions flow from a therapeutic worldview that says individuals are free from external moral authority and that personal feelings are the only proper source of individual choice. When it comes to making babies, the argument runs like this: Since our society permits unlimited reproductive freedom—whether or not to have children, when to have them, with whom to have them, and how many children to have—prospective parents should also be able to choose some of their children's characteristics.

This radical view of freedom has been described as "anti-culture" by sociologist Philip Rieff. The anti-culture mindset rejects any sacred or natural order that sets limits or gives direction to social arrangements. Thus, for the designer baby project, the issue is not about right and wrong. Rather, it is whether this or that technique will produce a child with the desired characteristics. Morality gives way to utility since the primary concern of anti-culture is how to achieve individual desires.

As the designer baby project amply illustrates, the spirit of anti-culture is ultimately anti-human. It rejects children who do not match parental desires. Only the Christian message of love—of one's neighbor (Mark 12:31), of the weak (James 1:27), of God and His created order (Deuteronomy 6:5–9)—is powerful enough to counter the distorted desires of the designer baby project. Love enables us to accept all children as unique and unrepeatable human beings. It envisions people, not projects. It liberates us to accept possibilities beyond our desires, even beyond our imaginations. Love enables sacrifice, even great sacrifice, without regard for loveliness and desirability. It is the embodiment of the very nature of God Himself.

14

So-Called Designer Baby Technology Can Exemplify Christian Principles

Gareth Jones

Gareth Jones is a professor at the University of Otago, New Zealand, in the Department of Anatomy. He is also the author of several books exploring the relationship between science and Christianity.

While the phrase "playing God" churns up negative connotations for many Christians, scientists who venture into the realm of genetic therapies have the opportunity to use new technologies for good. Terms like "designer babies," which raise concern within the Christian community, are often misnomers that conjure inaccurate pictures of what science seeks to and can accomplish. Even preimplantation genetic diagnosis, or PGD—a technique that allows for the screening of embryos before implantation into the womb—does not enable actual significant design. Since the embryos being screened already possess their God-given characteristics, scientists make choices much more than they create. Rather than worrying about scientists playing God, Christians should focus on the purposes to which genetic modification science is being put. Humankind has been given by God the power of creativity, and people should strive to use biotechnology to maintain and improve the dignity of human life.

The notion of playing God raises its ugly head in most scientific domains, the intended message being that this is forbidden territory. This is a term that is generally used negatively; it's usually a term of abuse. We are going where we should not be going. We are walking into an area that should be left to God. It's as though we are out on a walk, and ahead of us lies a field surrounded by a fence and a gate. There's no notice on the gate forbidding us from entering, but we assume that the fence by itself is enough to warn us that this is not somewhere we should wander. We should walk around the field or turn back. The field is God's field and we are mere human beings.

Not only this, but the word 'play' signifies a meddling with serious matters. We don't have to play, and we don't have to indulge in these activities. Not only are we entering forbidden territory but we are doing so needlessly. Life would be much safer if we left well alone; if we didn't play with fire. Why don't we accept that we are limited beings and that there are certain things outside our grasp?. . .

But what does the notion of 'playing God' actually mean; what does it signify? Is it nearly as negative and oppressive as frequently thought? The criticism that a procedure is akin to 'playing God' tends to reflect hostility towards the procedure rather than presenting a clear rationale as to the manner in which it transgresses divine boundaries. Many years ago, the theologian Paul Ramsey is said to have commented that human beings should not play God before they have learned to be human beings and when they are human beings they will not want to play God. While this makes a superb quotation, it fails to throw any light on what human beings should or should not do in any scientific area. The most one tends to elicit from such uses of the term, is that the present human form is divinely ordained and should not be modified in any manner, leaving in limbo the numerous uses made of vaccines, antibiotics, surgery, preventive medicine, and genetic counselling. Are these illicit illustrations of 'playing God' or do they manage to escape this opprobrium?

Using Science for Good

From a Christian standpoint we are made in God's image, and hence are to function like God. No matter how much our God-likeness has been shattered by sin and rebellion against God, we are still images of our maker, even if tarnished images. Consequently, we demonstrate a great deal of his creativity and his inquisitiveness. Humans as scientists are humans as God's images, probing and thrusting into the creation, attempting to understand it and re-direct it as stewards of God's creation. Within the medical sphere, the desire is to exercise at least limited control over evil in the form of diseases that would otherwise ravage and destroy all that is beautiful and worthy in God's world. Underlying all such attributes is a proviso, namely, that the control is exercised in a responsible manner.

When this is not the case, we see the other side of the picture, namely, that scientists may be arrogant and unworthy, with motives of self-aggrandisement and personal glory. They may show little regard for the welfare of individual humans, even when the realm within which they are working is that of medicine. Any attempt to create some new creature with superlative powers would stem from human conceit regarding the unlimited powers of human abilities. However, we should remind ourselves that this equates with playing the devil. It has nothing to do with playing God.

From a Christian perspective, we are not to use massive scientific powers for superficial and frivolous ends. There are always dangers, and to risk these for minor gains is dangerous and irresponsible. So much of the criticism of genetics revolves around its possible insubstantial uses, such as gene manipulation for eye colour or facial features. Such criticism is justified, but this is criticism of the misuse of genetics rather than of genetic advance itself. Similar criticism can be made of the misuse of many other technological developments, and even of human abilities themselves. Humans playing God only becomes dangerous when they fail to utilize their God-like capabilities in ways that will deepen and enrich the lives of human beings.

These negative images have to be taken seriously, and yet they fail to negate the overall thrust of much of scientific advance. Genetic advance per se is not synonymous with pride and arrogance. It is not an aping of God's power, since all forms of genetic therapy owe their rationale to this power. As long as the aim of therapy is the alleviation of human illness, it has the potential to elevate God's images. Nevertheless, there are always dangers, and the notion of 'playing God' should remind us that we are only to modify fundamental biological processes with enormous caution and deep humility. There is much we do not know, and there is much over which our control is tenuous and fragile at best. Playing God is an exercise in responsibility, demanding intelligence, compassion and spiritual discernment. It is not an exercise to be entered into frivolously. . . .

> *Humans playing God only becomes dangerous when they fail to utilize their God-like capabilities in ways that will deepen and enrich the lives of human beings.*

Babies Are Not Automobiles

The term designer babies is one of those terms beloved by sections of the media and popular press, and it is generally used negatively. Designing babies is one of the things we should not do, because it is going too far. For Christians this means it is doing something that should be left in the hands of God, where it rightfully belongs. No one with even a modicum of common sense, let alone spiritual discernment, would countenance the idea. It is playing God in the negative sense . . . , because the design of babies is a clear manifestation of playing God in a foolhardy manner.

In my view, dismissing bioethical issues in this way helps no one, and it certainly fails to answer any of the major ethical and theological questions that confront us with increasing vigour and complexity each week. We have to dig much deeper. Christians, in particular, should be searching for good reasons as to why they approve of some projects and disapprove of others. The last thing they should be content with are slogans.

The central problem with this debate is its unrealistic nature, based as it is on a set of misleading images of the notion of what designing a human being might entail, and on a serious lack of appreciation of the state of genetic science. . . .

Those who readily refer to designing babies are equally free in their references to 'making babies to order'. And if babies are made to order they will subsequently be treated as little more than impersonal products. After all, this is what design is all about; the more precise and sophisticated the design has been, the more effective and acceptable the product will be. Tell me what you want, and that is what you will be provided with. . . .

The production of a particular model of automobile is characterized by precision, equivalence and uniformity. There is no room for individuality on the production line, since each car has to conform to the specifications of that model. When I buy a car I expect it to perform exactly as all other examples of that particular model; the last thing I expect or want is for it to have interesting quirks of its own that no one had ever predicted and no one is capable of rectifying. Neither do I expect it to change its character as each year passes. To use a biological analogy its manufacture is entirely genetic in character; there is no environmental component, since no development can take place once it has come off the production line. Were the cloning of human beings or any genetic intervention to result in such reproducibility, we would be rightly alarmed. However, an environmental component is implicit in the production and subsequent development of all human beings—whether cloned or naturally fertilized, and it is this that separates human reproduction (even with impersonal elements) from factory manufacturing processes.

In this sense, biological manufacture is a misnomer. We will never produce babies in the same way as we produce cars, washing machines, or computers, even if we set out to do so. These analogies are, therefore, seriously misleading.

If design involves precision and predictability, there is no way in which babies and future human individuals will ever be designed by people like us. This in no way justifies all the procedures in the artificial reproductive technologies, but it should make us careful that we are not misled by the terminology we use.

Focus on Benefits for the Patient

What then about the science? Once again, there are problems. So often the focus appears to be on choosing genes for fair hair, blue eyes, intelligence, physique, and good looks, or avoiding baldness, or whatever. The ephemeral nature of these longings only serves to demonstrate their superficiality, let alone an ignorance of the scientific precision, clinical complexities and expensive resources that would be required to achieve them. Unfortunately, instead of demythologizing such fantasies as empty claims, they are taken seriously and are used to construct tirades against realistic and therapeutically based genetic choice. The latter can then be dismissed on the ground that its goal is that of producing perfect babies, designed to order. These twin themes of perfectibility and design carry powerful negative overtones, with their message that science is assuming redemptive powers; salvation can be found in biological manipulation, and the hope of a better life emanates from genetic intervention.

What is required is a rigorous assessment of the merits of what can and cannot be accomplished by genetic science. We need to ask what can be realistically accomplished to benefit the patient. This should be our starting point with its focus on the good of the patient, with a commitment to improve the quality of the patient's life and, if feasible, to replace illness by health. This is a positive hope, but it is also a realistic one. The genetic intervention may not work; hopes may be dashed. But the attempt is to be encouraged as long as our expectations are guided by realistic clinical and scientific goals. There is no hint here of perfection or of ageless existence in a disease-free body. The dominant value is that of humility, demonstrated by caring for those in need, and of utilizing powerful technologies in the service of those potentially capable of benefiting from them.

Even if design in a pure factory-production sense is not to be contemplated, where does this leave us when it comes to the genetic manipulation of embryos? This is much closer to a realistic view of where biomedical science is currently at, and also of how it may develop in the foreseeable future.

What is required is a rigorous assessment of the merits of what can and cannot be accomplished by genetic science.

Starting in the present-day, let's consider pre-implantation genetic diagnosis (PGD). This is a procedure devised to test early human embryos for serious inherited genetic conditions. Only embryos that are free from the condition are transferred to a woman, in the expectation that a normal pregnancy will develop. Inevitably, this involves selecting embryos: selecting those that are not genetic carriers of the disease trait, and discarding those that have the gene responsible for the disease. . . .

Choosing Is Not Designing

One of the features of PGD is that it enables the sex of embryos to be readily determined. This is both an advantage and a disadvantage. The advantage is that, when dealing with sex-linked genetic conditions such as hemophilia and Duchenne's muscular dystrophy, it enables embryos of the appropriate sex to be selected so that the resulting child will not suffer from the condition in question. This is exactly what is required. The disadvantage is that sex selection can be used for spurious social control of the next generation by providing parents with a child of the preferred sex. This form of sex selection may have nothing to do with anything medical or therapeutic.

Some people refer to babies born after PGD as designer babies, since there is interference at a very early stage of their development. In my view this is not design in any meaningful sense, even though choices are being made between embryos. But, in terms of design, the choice is a crude one. Whenever I buy a jacket and decide that this jacket is preferable to that jacket, I have not suddenly become a clothes designer. All I have done is make a selection from the two that are available. PGD is similar, even if somewhat more sophisticated. The design component is negligible. Of course, we do not have to travel in this direction, and PGD does not have to be undertaken. However, once an appropriate procedure is available, choices are inevitably being made, even if the decision is to refrain from utilizing the procedure. . . .

Genetic modification brought about by humans, genetic design, if you like, has the potential for extending the work of God.

How Christians Can Contribute to the Debate

In the end what is crucial is the welfare of the individuals concerned. The determining question is always to be: what will uphold human dignity and human value—both now and in the future?

This discussion has pointed to a place for design within genetics and other biomedical areas, but design of a far more limited and humble variety than so often encountered in these debates. It is far removed from the bravado and hubris associated with the picture of a factory production line of identical and preordained babies. The challenge is to determine how we do these things, and under what circumstances we do them, because this is where responsibility, judgement and discernment come into play. We can't do anything we like; we shouldn't do anything we like. But we should do all we can to improve the quality of the lives of those around us, whether by using biological means or simply by treating them as beings of importance and as people who matter.

This it seems to me is where Christians should be contributing to this debate. If we consider that God is sovereign over all, he is sovereign over the genetic realm, just as he is over human life, human community, and the ecosphere. Divine grace and creativity are evident in all these realms, and human creativity is to follow suit. If we can say that God works through creation and, therefore, through what we describe as the natural world, there is no reason to say that he does not also work through the basic processes described by biology and, therefore, through genetic and allied mechanisms. If this is true, we can go on to say that genetic modification brought about by humans, genetic design if you like, has the potential for extending the work of God. Of course, this has enormous dangers and pitfalls, since appallingly injudicious choices can be made, but this is true of every other area of human life.

Humility is essential for rigorously assessing the merits of what can and cannot be accomplished by genetic science. Using the therapeutic and person-centred framework I have advocated, our eyes can be directed towards what can realistically be accomplished to benefit the patient. . . .

We are to do what is consistent with the nature and purposes of God, and are to assess all scientific developments by the benchmark of whether they appear to forward God's work in creation. Daunting as these tasks are, and inadequate as we are to tackle them, they are enriched when theological, scientific and ethical insights are brought to bear on them in an integrated fashion.

Organizations to Contact

The editors have compiled the following list of organizations concerned with the issues debated in this book. The descriptions are derived from materials provided by the organizations. All have publications or information available for interested readers. The list was compiled on the date of publication of the present volume; names, addresses, phone and fax numbers, and e-mail and Internet addresses may change. Be aware that many organizations take several weeks or longer to respond to inquiries, so allow as much time as possible.

The Center for Research on Reproduction and Women's Health

3701 Market St. #3, Philadelphia, PA   19104
(215) 662-6100
website: www.pennmedicine.org/fertility/

The Center for Research on Reproduction and Women's Health, part of the Perelman School of Medicine at the University of Pennsylvania, conducts clinical trials and research on fertility and women's health issues, aiming to increase the understanding of human reproduction. Clinical services include preimplantation genetic diagnosis (PGD), used to screen for genetic or chromosomal disorders.

Centre for Preimplantation Genetic Diagnosis

Guy's Hospital, Tower Wing, 11th Floor, London   SE1 9RT
(020) 7188 1364 (UK Number)
email: PGDGenetic@qstt.nhs.uk
website: www.pgd.org.uk

The Centre for Preimplantation Genetic Diagnosis is a London-based clinic that has garnered an international reputation as being a leader in preimplantation genetic diagnosis (PGD) services.

The Fertility Institutes of Los Angeles
Los Angeles Office, Encino, CA   91436
(818) 728-4600
email: TZFertility@aol.com
website: www.fertility-docs.com

The Fertility Institutes, founded in 1986, is a clinic that provides a variety of fertility services including in-vitro fertilization (IVF), preimplantation genetic diagnosis (PGD), gender selection, fertility and sperm evaluations, and egg-freezing programs. The clinic also participates in new advances in fertility science.

The Human Fertilisation and Embryology Authority
Finsbury Tower, London   EC1Y 8HF
(020) 7291-8200
email: admin@hfea.gov.uk
website: www.hfea.gov.uk

The Human Fertilisation and Embryology Authority is the United Kingdom's independent regulator of fertility treatments and research, issuing standards and licenses to clinics and providing policy for complex fertility issues.

Mount Sinai School of Medicine Department of Genetics and Genomics
One Gustave L. Levy Place, New York, NY   10029
(212) 241-6500
email: multiscale.biology@mssm.edu
website: www.mssm.edu/departments-and-institutes/genetics -and-genomic-sciences

The Mount Sinai Department of Genetics and Genomic Sciences is one of the largest genetics centers in the United States and provides, among many diagnostic services, ethnicity-based carrier screenings and prenatal diagnosis.

The National Human Genome Research Institute
National Institutes of Health, Bethesda, MD   20892
(301) 402-0911
website: www.genome.gov

The National Human Genome Research Institute, originally the Center for Human Genome Research (NCHGR), was established as the enactor of the National Institutes of Health's role in the Human Genome Project (HGP). The HGP began in 1990 with the mission of mapping the human genome and later expanded to include the application of genome technology to the study of disease.

The National Society of Genetic Counselors

401 N. Michigan Avenue, 22nd Floor, Chicago, IL   60611
(312) 321-6834
email: nsgc@nsgc.org
website: www.nsgc.org

The National Society of Genetic Counselors (NSGC) provides a network for communication between professionals and those seeking genetic counseling and works to support the advancement of genetics and genomics in the health care system through public policy.

The New York Genome Center

590 Madison Avenue, 21st Floor, New York, NY   10022
(888) 415-6942
email: info@nygenome.org
website: www.nygenome.org

The New York Genome Center (NYGC) is a nonprofit, independent organization that aims to ally the resources of medical centers, universities, and for-profit organizations to advance the study of genomics and develop new means of diagnosing and treating genetic diseases.

Bibliography

Books

Critical Art
Ensemble
Flesh Machine: Cyborgs, Designer Babies, and New Eugenic Consciousness. Brooklyn: Autonomedia, 1998.

Sarah Franklin
and Celia Roberts
Born and Made: An Ethnography of Preimplantation Genetic Diagnosis. Princeton: Princeton University Press, 2006.

Joel Garreau
Radical Evolution: The Promise and Peril of Enhancing Our Minds, Our Bodies—and What It Means to Be Human. New York: Broadway Books, 2006.

Masha Gessen
Blood Matters: From Inherited Illness to Designer Babies, How the World and I Found Ourselves in the Future of the Gene. Boston: Houghton Mifflin Harcourt, 2009.

Ronald
Michael Green
Babies by Design: The Ethics of Genetic Choice. New Haven: Yale University Press, 2007.

Matti Hayry
The Ethics and Governance of Human Genetic Databases: European Perspectives. Cambridge and New York: Cambridge University Press, 2007.

Steve Jones   *Genetics in Medicine: Real Promises,*
                     Unreal Expectations: One Scientist's
                     Advice to Policymakers in the United
                     Kingdom and the United States. New
                     York: Milbank Memorial Fund, 2000.

Ray Kurzweil   *The Singularity Is Near: When*
                     Humans Transcend Biology. New
                     York: Penguin, 2006.

Rose M. Morgan   *The Genetics Revolution: History,*
                     Fears, and Future of a Life-Altering
                     Science. Westport, CT: Greenwood
                     Press, 2006.

Spencer S. Stober   *God, Science, and Designer Genes: An*
                     Exploration of Emerging Genetic
                     Technologies. Santa Barbara,
                     California: Praeger, 2009.

Colin Tudge   *The Impact of the Gene: From*
                     Mendel's Peas to Designer Babies. New
                     York: Hill and Wang, 2001.

Laura R. Wolier   *The Political Geographies of*
                     Pregnancy. Urbana, IL: University of
                     Illinois Press, 2002.

Periodicals and Internet Sources

Nicholas Agar   "Designer Babies: Ethical
                     Considerations," Action Bioscience,
                     April 2006. http://www.actionbio
                     science.org/biotech/agar.html.

Dilly Barlow   "Life and Death in the 21ˢᵗ Century:
                      Designer Babies," BBC2—Horizon,
                      January 6, 2000. http://www.bbc.co
                      .uk/science/horizon/1999/designer
                      _babies_script.shtml.

Bionet Online   "What Is a Designer Baby?," 2002.
                      http://www.bionetonline.org
                      /English/Content/db_cont1.htm.

Robert Roy Britt   "Designer Babies: Ethical?
                      Inevitable?," LiveScience, January 11,
                      2009. http://www.livescience.com
                      /3213-designer-babies-ethical
                      -inevitable.html.

Andy Coghlan   "Will Designer Brains Divide
                      Humanity?," *New Scientist*, May 13,
                      2009. http://www.newscientist
                      .com/article/mg20227083.700
                      -will-designer-brains divide
                      -humanity.html.

Future   "Genetic Engineering: Designer
Human Evolution   Babies," 2010. http://www.humans
                      future.org/genetic_engineering
                      _designer_babies.php.htm.

Human   "Genetic Enhancement Can Not Be a
Advancement   Bad Thing," October 10, 2008.
and Biopolitics   http://hplusbiopolitics.wordpress
                      .com/2008/10/10/genetic-enhancement
                      -can-not-be-a-bad-thin/.

Ellie Lee	"Debating 'Designer Babies,' Personal Reproductive Choices Should Not Be a Matter for Legal Regulation," Spiked Science Online, April 17, 2003. http://www.spiked-online .com/articles/00000006DD57.htm.
Michigan News Live	"Our Turn: Would Engineering Designer Babies Be Unethical?," October 30, 2010. http://www.mlive .com/opinion/kalamazoo/index.ssf /2010/10/our_turn_would_engineering _des.html.
Gautam Naik	"A Baby, Please. Blond, Freckles—Hold the Colic," *Wall Street Journal*, February 12, 2009. http://online.wsj.com/article /SB123439771603075099.html.
Plausible Futures Newsletter	"The Future of Designer Babies," April 7, 2007. http://plausiblefutures .wordpress.com/2007/04/07/the-future -of-designer-babies/.
Leslie A. Pray	"Embryo Screening and the Ethics of Human Genetic Engineering," *Nature Education*, 2008. http://www.nature .com/scitable/topicpage/Embryo -Screening-and-the-Ethics-of-60561.
Yin Ren	"Designer Babies: The Pros and Cons of Genetic Engineering," *Massachusetts Institute of Technology Undergraduate Research Journal*, Spring 2005. http://web.mit.edu /murj/www/v12/v12-Features/v12-f4 .pdf.

Rebecca Sato   "The First GM Human Embryo
                        Could Dramatically Alter the Future,"
                        The Daily Galaxy, March 20, 2009.
                        http://www.dailygalaxy.com/my
                        _weblog/2009/03/the-worlds-fi-1.html.

Mike Steere   "Designer Babies: Creating the
                        Perfect Child," CNN Online, October
                        30, 2008. http://articles.cnn.com
                        /2008-10-30/tech/designer.babies_1
                        _designer-babies-perfect-child-genetic
                        -screening?_s=PM:TECH.

Gregory Stock   "Humans: Objects of Conscious
                        Design," BBC2—Horizon, 1999.
                        http://www.bbc.co.uk/science
                        /horizon/1999/stock.shtml.

Robert Taylor   "Superhumans: Like It or Not, In a
                        Few Short Years We'll Have the
                        Power to Control Our Own
                        Evolution," Center for Genetics and
                        Society, October 1, 1998. http://www
                        .geneticsandsociety.org/article.php?id
                        =129.

Index

A

Aging, importance of, 53–54, 75
American Society for Reproductive Medicine (ASRM), 20, 34
Anti-culture mindset, 85
Austadt, Steven, 54

B

Biogerontology goals, 54
Biotechnology. *See* Medical technology
"Book of Life" (human DNA sequence), 52
Brave New World (Huxley), 7, 46–47, 66
Build-a-Bear babies, 12, 33

C

Capitalism, 73–74
Celizic, Mike, 14
Children as commodities or gifts, 12
Cho, Hemmy, 41
Christian Science Monitor (newspaper), 11
Christianity
    fundamentalism, 59
    human nature, 88
    principle of love, 85
    use of science, 88–89, 92, 94–95
Cloning of humans
    achievement of reproducibility, 13, 90–91
    is inevitable, 59–60

media hype, 56
reasons for banning, 71, 75
"Code of Codes" (human DNA sequence), 52
Commodities, children as, 12
Cosmetic conditions
    line separating from health conditions, 39
    market exists for selection, 25
    pharmacology, 55
    public opinion opposes use of PGD, 8, 9
    quality of life, 39
    trait selection for, 21, 24–26, 91
Costs, 15–16, 48

D

Darnovsky, Marcy, 16, 27
Dawkins, Richard, 42
Deafness, congenital, 8–9, 82–83
Death, importance of, 71–72
DeCode Genetics of Iceland, 25
Deliberate selection vs. natural selection, 12
Designer babies
    defined, 7, 48
    future possibility of, 20–21
    selection vs., 93
    term is misleading, 89–90, 91
DNA
    advances in, allow trait selection, 25
    is not sum total of humans, 13, 90–91
Duchesneau, Sharon, 8–9, 83, 84